THE PROBLEM OF THE LITURGICAL REFORM

A Theological and Liturgical Study

The Society of Saint Pius X

ANGELUS PRESS
2918 TRACY AVENUE,
KANSAS CITY, MISSOURI 64109

Library of Congress Cataloging-in-Publication Data

Problème de la réforme liturgique. English.
  The problem of the liturgical reform : Mass of Vatican II
    and of Paul VI : a theological and liturgical study.-- 1st ed.
    p. cm.
  Includes bibliographical references.
  ISBN 1-892331-09-8
  1. Catholic Church. Ordo Missae. 2. Catholic Church. General
instruction of the Roman missal. 3. Lord's Supper-- Sacrifice.
4. Lord's Supper--Catholic Church. 5. Mass.
I. Title.

BX2218 .P7613
264'.36--dc21

                                            2001034138

ANGELUS PRESS

2918 TRACY AVENUE
KANSAS CITY, MISSOURI 64109
PHONE (816) 753-3150
FAX (816) 753-3557
ORDER LINE 1-800-966-7337

ISBN 1-892331-09-8
FIRST PRINTING—July 2001

Printed in the United States of America

CONTENTS

PART ONE

PART TWO

BISHOP FELLAY'S LETTER TO POPE JOHN PAUL II

Holy Father,

More than thirty years ago, under your predecessor, Pope Paul VI, a major reform modified the Latin rite of the Catholic liturgy, especially the "Order of the Mass."

This reform immediately raised troubles and controversies across the entire world. Some studies which were made, notably the "Brief Critical Examination of the *Novus Ordo Missae*" given to Pope Paul VI by Cardinals Ottaviani and Bacci, pointed out the troubling deficiencies and ambiguities affecting this reform.

The liturgy has certainly evolved over the course of history, as is shown by the reforms made during the past century by St. Pius X, Pius XII and John XXIII. But the post-conciliar liturgical reform, by its extension and brutality, represents a disturbing upheaval, as a radical rupture from the traditional Roman liturgy. Above all, this reform contains disconcerting elements, ambiguous and dangerous for the Faith.

Before this spiritual danger, the true obedience to the Seat of Peter, the true submission to the Church Mother and Mistress obliges us, along with a great number of Catholics around the world, to remain faithful, no matter the cost, to this venerable liturgy which the Roman Church has celebrated for centuries, the liturgy which you yourself have celebrated in the past. Such is the sacred heritage which the founder of our Priestly Fraternity of Saint Pius X, Archbishop Lefebvre, has entrusted to us: "It is clear, it is evident that the entire drama between Ecône and Rome is due to the problem of the Mass....We are convinced that the new rite of Mass expresses a new Faith, a Faith which is not ours, a Faith which is not the Catholic Faith;...that this new rite is misleading and, if I may say, supposes another conception of the Catholic Religion....This is why we are attached to this Tradition which is expressed in such an admirable manner, and in a definitive manner, as Pope Saint Pius V said so well, in the Sacrifice of the Mass" (June 29, 1976).

After much reflection and prayer, we feel the duty before God to address Your Holiness once again with regard to this problem of the liturgy. We have asked those pastors of souls who are qualified in theological, liturgical and canonical matters, to compose a synthesis of the certain difficulties, including the most important ones, which the liturgy of the post-conciliar reform poses to the faith of Catholics.

This work has sought to go back to the doctrinal causes properly so-called of the actual crisis, bringing to light the principles which are at the origin of the liturgical reform and contrasting them with Catholic doctrine.

The reading of this document manifests clearly, we believe, that the "theology of the Paschal mystery," to which the door was left open at the occasion of Vatican II, is the soul of the liturgical reform. Because it minimizes the mystery of the Redemption, because it considers the sacrament only in its relation with the "mystery," and because the conception that it makes of the "memorial" alters the sacrificial dimension of the Mass, this "theology of the Paschal mystery" renders the post-conciliar liturgy dangerously distant from Catholic doctrine, to which, however, the Christian conscience remains bound forever.

Holy Father, the Catholic Faith imposes upon us a grave obligation of not remaining silent about the questions which assail our mind.

Are not the deficiencies of this theology and of the liturgy which issues from it one of the principal causes of the crisis affecting the Church for more than 30 years? And does not such a situation demand the doctrinal and liturgical clarifications on the part of the supreme Authority of the Church? Do not the subjects, for whose good a law is made, have the right and duty, if the law manifests itself harmful, with filial confidence to demand from the legislator its modification or its abrogation?

Among the measures which are the most urgent, does it not seem appropriate to make publicly known that every priest possesses the faculty to use the integral and fruitful Roman Missal revised by Saint Pius V, a treasure so profoundly rooted in the thousand-year Tradition of the Church, Mother and Mistress?

These doctrinal and liturgical clarifications, joined with the universal renewal of the traditional Roman liturgy, would not fail to produce immense spiritual fruits: the restoration of the true notion of the priesthood and of sacrifice, and consequently, the renewal of priestly and religious sanctity; the increase of fervor in the faithful; the strengthening of the unity of the Church; the powerful momentum for the evangelization of former Christian nations and of infidel nations.

We strongly beseech Your Holiness, who alone has the power as Successor of Peter and Shepherd of the universal Church, to strengthen his brethren in the Faith and to sanction with his apostolic authority the indispensable clarifications which are demanded by the present tragic situation in the Church.

However, such a necessary restoration cannot be done in the Church without an extraordinary recourse to the Holy Ghost, obtained by the intercession of the Blessed Virgin Mary. It is, therefore, by prayer, especially by the Holy Sacrifice of the Mass, that this long-desired renewal will be accomplished, and, for our part, it is to this, with the grace of God, that we give ourselves and desire to give ourselves always more.

Deign, Your Holiness, to accept our sentiments of filial respect in Jesus and Mary.

Bishop Bernard Fellay
Superior General
Priestly Fraternity of Saint Pius X
(Flavigny, France, Feast of the
Presentation of the Lord, Feb. 2, 2001)

FOREWORD

While this study goes to the very root of the problem with the liturgical reforms, the analysis will focus for reasons of clarity on the Missal of Pope Paul VI. The Mass is, after all, the jewel in the crown of the Catholic Liturgy.

Three theses introduce, in turn, the three parts of the study. *Firstly*, we will show how the publication of the New Mass of 1969 constituted a liturgical rupture. *Secondly*, we will show how that rupture is chiefly explained by a new theology of the Redemption, which we will call the "Theology of the Paschal Mystery." This complex second part forms the very heart of our study. *Thirdly*, we will seek to evaluate the new theology in the light of the infallible teachings of the Church, and to establish what attitude one should have towards this *Novus Ordo Missae*. In support of this attitude, an appendix (see Part III, Chapter 3, pp.95*ff*) treating the canonical status and rights of the Mass of St. Pius V is attached.

By no means exhaustive, this study gets to the central issue at stake; the official texts show quite categorically that the "Paschal mystery" is the key to interpreting the entire Liturgical Reform.

ABBREVIATIONS USED

BAC   *Biblioteca de Autores Cristianos,* Madrid.

CCC   *Catechism of the Catholic Church,* (The Wanderer Press, 1994).

DC   *La Documentation catholique,* journal of a Catholic news service, Bayard Press.

DS   Denzinger-Schönmetzer, *Enchiridion Symbolorum Definitionum et Declarationum de Rebus Fidei et Morum,* 36th ed. (Herder, 1976).

Dz.   *The Sources of Catholic Dogma,* tr. by Roy J. Deferrari from the 30th Edition of Henry Denzinger's *Enchiridion Symbolorum,* (St. Louis: B. Herder Book Co., 1957).

IG   *Institutio Generalis Missalis Romani.* Unless specified otherwise, the original version of 1969 is cited. [English translations taken from *Vatican Council II: The Conciliar and Post Conciliar Documents,* Austin Flannery, O.P., General Editor, (Collegeville, MN: The Liturgical Press, 1975), unless otherwise noted.]

JLW   *Jahrbuch fur Liturgieswissenschaft.*

LMD   *La Maison-Dieu,* a pastoral and liturgical review (Ed. le Cerf)

NDL   *Nuovo dizionario di liturgia,* ed. Domenico Sartore and Achille M. Triacca (San Paolo, 1988)

Unless otherwise stated: In citations, the italics have been added for emphasis. Quotations from foreign language texts have been translated by the authors, except where authorized versions of official documents exist (Vatican Council II, encyclicals, *etc.*). [For this English version, quotations from authors have been translated from the French text, except where published English versions exist; in this case, the reference to the published source is provided.]

PART ONE

THE REFORM OF 1969: A LITURGICAL RUPTURE

THESIS

1. On Maundy Thursday, April 3, 1969, Pope Paul VI signed the Apostolic Constitution *Missale Romanum* and gave the Church in the West a reformed missal. In so doing he acted upon the decisions of the Second Vatican Council which declared in the constitution *Sacrosanctum Concilium*: "In order that the Christian people may more certainly derive an abundance of graces from the sacred liturgy, holy Mother Church desires to undertake with great care a general restoration of the liturgy itself" (§21). The regulation of the liturgy (and therefore of its possible reform) does indeed belong exclusively to the authority of the Church, *i.e.,* to the Holy See and, according to the prescriptions of Canon Law and by delegation, to the bishops. In order, however, for Catholics to nourish their spiritual lives through the liturgy, they must be able to find in the rites the authentic teachings of the Magisterium of the Church. "But if one desires to differentiate and describe the relationship between faith and the sacred Liturgy in absolute and general terms, it is perfectly correct to say: '*Lex credendi legem statuat supplicandi*—let the rule of belief determine the rule of prayer.'"[1]

2. In its 23rd Session, the Council of Trent reminds us of the doctrines concerning the Mass which the Catholic Faith obliges us to hold. In instituting the Eucharist, Christ left us *a true sacrifice*:

    (a) "...nevertheless, that His sacerdotal office might not come to an end with His death, at the Last Supper, on the night He was betrayed, so that He might leave to His beloved spouse the Church a visible sacrifice (as the

---

[1]   Pius XII, *Mediator Dei.*

nature of man demands)…[He offered to God the Father His own body and blood under the species of bread and wine.…]" DS 1740 (Dz. 938).

(b) In this sacrifice Christ renews in an unbloody manner the immolation He offered on the Cross when He presented Himself to the Eternal Father as an acceptable victim. This sacrifice is the sacrifice of the Cross itself since *the priest and the victim are identical:* "For, it is one and the same Victim, the same one now offering by the ministry of the priests as He who then offered Himself on the Cross, the manner of offering alone being different" (DS 1743).

(c) Since the sacrifice of the Cross was offered for the remission of our sins (Heb. 9:28) the Holy Sacrifice of the Mass has a propitiatory aim. "And since in this divine sacrifice, which is celebrated in the Mass, that same Christ is contained and immolated in an unbloody manner, who on the altar of the Cross 'once offered Himself' in a bloody manner, the holy Synod teaches that this is truly propitiatory…" (*ibid.*). The Council adds: "The fruits of that oblation (bloody, that is) are received most abundantly through this unbloody one…" (*ibid.*).

These doctrinal principles concerning the Mass are indispensable to the Faith, and we are entitled to find them when analyzing these rites.

3. The analysis of the new missal must be based on a joint study of the *Novus Ordo Missae* and of the *Institutio Generalis Missalis Romani* [abbreviated IG] which prefaces the missal of 1969. In fact:

> The new missal is prefaced by a General Introduction (*Institutio Generalis*) which, far from being a mere collection of rubrics, is a synthesis of theological, ascetical and pastoral principles. These are essential to the knowledge of the faith, as to the celebration of the Mass, and the catechetics and pastoral practices underpinning it.[2]

---

[2] *Lettre pontificale à la semaine liturgique d'Italie,* DC 1594, Oct.3, 1971, p.866.

As such, the document was distributed[3] and welcomed.[4] The clarifications included in the 1970 edition did not change the text substantially since, "when the members and experts of the Consilium examined the General Instruction, both before and after its publication, they found no doctrinal error and no reason to make any changes."[5] We will, nevertheless, indicate as and when necessary, where these clarifications were made.[6]

4. The analysis of the *Novus Ordo Missae* and the *Institutio Generalis Missalis Romani* compels us to recognize that the struc-

---

[3] *Cf. Notitiae* 40, 1968, p.181: "It concerns theological principles and pastoral and rubrical norms for the celebration of the Mass." Annibale Bugnini, "Report given to the second general meeting of the Latin American Episcopate," *Revista Eclesiastica Brasileira*, 1968, p.628: "[It is] a full theological, pastoral, catechetical and rubrical exposé: it is an introduction to understanding and celebrating the Mass." *Cf. Notitiae* 46, April 1969, p.151: *Introduction to the New Missal*, DC 1541, June 1, 1969, p.518. If, in the face of criticism, the Congregation for Divine Worship had to examine again the theological value of the "Introduction" (*Changes made to the General Introduction to the New Mass,* DC 1568, Aug. 2, 1970), it was to approve the document when the objections died down: "The theology and discipline of the sacraments have been clearly exposed in the *Praenotanda* of various recently published rites. For the Mass the *Institutio Generalis Missalis Romani* is an exposé concerning the Eucharist" (Reply of the Congregation for Divine Worship, *Notitiae* 81, March 1973, p.101).

[4] *Cf. Official Instructions concerning the New Rites of Mass*, CNPL, (Centurion 1969), p.10; Rober Cabié, "Le Nouvel *Ordo missae*," LMD 100, 4th Trimester 1969, p.22; F. Sottocornala, "*Il nuovo Ordo Poenitentiae*," *Notitiae*, 90, February 1974, p.67; Adrien Nocent, "La celebration de l'Eucharistie avant et après saint Pie V," *Nouvelle révue théologique*, Jan.-Feb. 1977, p.19 [Nocent was a member of the *Consilium* for the Congregation for Divine Worship.]; Aimé-Georges Martimort, *L'Eglise en prière*, (Desclée, 1983), Vol. I, p.5 [Martimort was a member of the *Consilium* for the Congregation for Divine Worship.], *etc.*

[5] *Modifications apportées à la Présentation générale du missel romain*, DC 1568, August 2, 1970, p.170. *Cf. Déclaration de la Congrégation pour le Culte divin au sujet de la 'Présentation générale' du missel romain*, DC 1558, March 1, 1970, p.215: "A careful study of this 'General Introduction' very clearly shows that the doubts and negative criticisms vehemently made of its doctrine are completely without foundation."

[6] The 2000 edition of the *Institutio Generalis Missalis Romani* comes from the same theological stable as previous editions and does not change substantially the judgments made here. Moreover, it is linked to a new edition of the missal which has not yet been published, and so it is not taken into account by the present study.

ture of the rite is no longer based on sacrifice but on a memorial meal (Chapter 1). We will also see that this rite has emphasized the presence of Christ in His Word and in his people, and has diminished the importance of the presence of Christ as Priest and Victim (Chapter 2). Consequently, the Eucharistic dimension has become more significant than the propitiatory aim (Chapter 3). The inevitable conclusion of these observations is that the expression "liturgical rupture" defines the differences between the traditional missal[7] and the new missal more accurately than the expression "liturgical reform." The causes underlying these innovations will be explored in Part Two.

---

[7] For editorial reasons, we will call the missal published in 1969 the *new missal* to distinguish it from the *traditional missal* whose last edition was published in 1962.

CHAPTER 1

FROM SACRIFICE TO MEMORIAL MEAL

5. A comparison of the missal revised by St. Pius V and the missal of Paul VI at first shows certain likenesses between the two orders of Mass; an opening rite, *Kyrie Eleison, Gloria,* readings and *Credo,* preparation of the offerings on the altar, Preface and *Sanctus,* Consecration, *Pater Noster,* distribution of Communion. A closer analysis reveals, however, that despite the material appearances remaining the same, the structure of the Eucharistic liturgy has been changed at its very foundations. In place of the sacrificial structure of the traditional missal—oblation, consecration, consummation—the new missal has substituted the structure of the Jewish meal—*berakah* or blessing of the food, thanksgiving for gifts received, and the breaking and partaking, of bread.

I. THE STRUCTURE OF THE TRADITIONAL MISSAL: A SACRIFICE

6. Since the Mass is a true sacrifice in which He who offered Himself in a bloody manner on the Cross (DS 1743), offers Himself in an unbloody manner, the Tradition of the Church has clearly shown "the sacrifice of this pure oblation" (Mal. 1:11) by means of an explicitly sacrificial rite. Since man is not capable, however, of instantly comprehending all the riches of the sacrificial action wrought by the words of consecration, the light of this unique mystery will shine forth in the liturgical rites, which are designed to reveal its innermost truths and make us partake of them.

7. The Roman Missal has thus assumed the essential form of sacrifice seen in the sacrifices of the Old Testament: oblation of the victim (Offertory), immolation (double consecration), consummation (Communion). In order, however, that men may see in this ritual progression a reflection of the unique, sacrificial act,

the liturgy has always relied upon one most enlightening practice, *i.e.*, even before the Consecration, the bread and wine are already treated as the immolated divine Body and Blood.[8] Likewise, after the Consecration the liturgy boldly treats the bread and wine as if they were not yet consecrated.[9] This anticipatory, liturgical practice explains, for example, the beautiful words of the Offertory: "Receive, O holy Father, this spotless host"; "We offer you, O Lord, the Chalice of Salvation." In view of this practice and structure, the Mass is seen to be a unified, sacrificial action which is premeditated, offered, accomplished, adored and glorified, and finally consummated in the unity of the Mystical Body.

II. THE STRUCTURE OF THE NEW MISSAL: A MEMORIAL MEAL

8. Some promoters of the pastoral liturgy have thought that when Christ instituted the Eucharist during the paschal meal, He was adopting the memorial aspect of the Jewish Passover and leaving aside its sacrificial dimension.[10] The link between the Mass and the Cross is thereby diminished, and its links with the Last Supper emphasized. The Liturgical Reform shares the vision advocated by these modernizers. The *Institutio Generalis Missali Romani*, §2, associates the Mass with the "celebration of the Supper of the Lord" where Christ "instituted the Eucharistic sacrifice of his Body and Blood. He did this in order to perpetuate the sacrifice of the Cross until he should come again; and he wished to entrust to his beloved Spouse, the Church, a memorial of his death and resurrection." Since Christ, therefore, performed the ritual acts of a Jewish meal on Maundy Thursday, those acts will, henceforth, define the structure of the Mass: *berakah* or blessing of the food (presentation of the gifts), thanksgiving for gifts re-

---

8   Pierre le Brun, *Explication de la Messe*, collection *Lex orandi* (Paris: Cerf, 1949), p.277. At the *Te igitur* mention is already made of certain *sacrificia illibata*. In the Common of the Saints of the traditional missal, the *orationes super oblata* or "secrets" use the term *hostia* 31 times, the term *sacrificium* 39 times, and the term *immolatio* four times.

9   See for example, the Eastern *epiclesis*.

10   Henrie-Marie Férét, *La messe, rassemblement de la communauté*, collection *Lex orandi*, (Paris: Cerf, 1947), 227-230. Louis Bouyer, *Eucharistie* (Desclée, 1990), p.103. [Bouyer was a member of the *Consilium* and of the International Theological Commission.]

ceived (Eucharistic prayer), breaking and partaking of the bread (IG §48).

9. Thus, in place of the Offertory, the architects of the new missal thought they ought to "place what we call today the 'words of institution' of the Eucharist back into their own context which is that of the ritual *berakoth* of the Jewish meal…"[11] At the heart of the new "Presentation of the Gifts" will be prayers "in part borrowed word for word from the Jewish grace-before-meals"[12]:

> Blessed are you, Lord, God of all creation. Through your goodness we have this bread to offer, which earth has given and human hands have made. It will become for us the bread of life.

These words of thanksgiving ("Blessed are you") are orientated towards the paschal meal ("It will become for us the Bread of Life") and have replaced the words from the traditional missal: "Accept, O holy Father, almighty and eternal God, this unspotted host, which I, Thy unworthy servant, offer unto Thee, my living and true God, for my innumerable sins, offenses, and negligences, and for all here present: as also for all faithful Christians, both living and dead, that it may avail both me and them for salvation unto life everlasting."

The tenor of sacrifice which characterized the Tridentine Offertory has thus disappeared from the "Presentation of the Gifts": the Tridentine Offertory states that the sacrifice (the word is used four times) is offered for our sins (*Suscipe sancte Pater*), since by our contrition, we want to be separated from other sinners (*Lavabo*). We offer to God, therefore, the immaculate host (*Suscipe sancte Pater*) and the chalice of salvation (*Offerimus*) participating in the Redemption wrought by Jesus Christ (*Deus, qui humanae* and *Suscipe sancta Trinitas*) while relying on the intercession of the saints (*Suscipe sancta Trinitas*). We humbly implore God in His mercy (*In spiritu humilitatis*) to accept (*ibid.*) this sacrifice for the glory of His name (*Veni Sanctificator; Suscipe sancta Trinitas*) so that it may obtain salvation (*Suscipe sancte Pater; Offerimus; Suscipe sancta Trinitas*) both for the living and the dead (*Suscipe sancte*

---

[11] Louis Bouyer, *op. cit.,* p.109.
[12] Letter of Cardinal Hoeffner to the priests of the Archdiocese of Chicago, DC 1686, November 16, 1975, p.983.

Pater). These numerous allusions no longer feature in the new "Presentation of the Gifts." We too can state with official commentators, "We have gone from an offertory in the strict sense of the word to a simple presentation of gifts which will become 'the bread of life and the cup of salvation.'"[13]

10. By becoming the "Eucharistic Prayer," the Canon has also been greatly affected, even if the appearance of the rite seems more or less similar. Since at the Last Supper Christ took bread and gave thanks, the *Institutio Generalis Missalis Romani* presents this part of the Mass as a "prayer of thanksgiving and consecration" (IG §54) akin to the thanksgiving prayers which accompany ritual Jewish meals (CCC §1328). The plan of this part is also explained: "The meaning of the prayer is that all the faithful now gathered together unite themselves with Christ in praising the wonderful works of God and in offering sacrifice" (IG §54). The offering of the sacrifice will, therefore, follow a calling to mind of the great works of God.

11. The first part of the Eucharistic Prayer is an offering of thanksgiving which acts as a setting for the formulae of consecration. These latter are understood as an *account* of the institution of the Eucharist (IG §55d). If Eucharistic Prayer IV shows this pattern most clearly, the other Eucharistic Prayers are nonetheless marked by it: "In the Eucharistic Prayer, God is thanked for the whole work of redemption, and the gifts become the Body and Blood of Christ" (Flannery ed., p.174, IG §48b). The double consecration is then relegated to the background, and smacks more of an act of remembrance than of sacrifice: it concerns rather a past action already accomplished than the making present of any effect. Yet the change in emphasis from the pre-eminence of the sacrifice to that of the memorial meal is manifested above all by the modifications made to the words of consecration.

● Firstly, in the traditional missal the words "Take and eat this all of you," "Take and drink this all of you" are clearly

---

13   J. M. Martin Patino, A. Pardo, A. Iniesta and P. Farnes, *Nuevas normas de la missa*, BAC, 1969, p.125. [Patino was a member of the *Consilium*.]

separated from the words of consecration. In the new missal, however, they are incorporated into the very form of the sacrament. Thus at the heart of the liturgical action the aspect of friendship is emphasized.

● Following the consecration of the host, the expression found in Lk. 22:19, "delivered for you," has been introduced. This reference to the Passion of Christ at the first consecration takes away the sacrificial dimension found in the words of consecration in the traditional missal. By not mentioning the Passion until the consecration of the chalice, the traditional missal shows that the separate consecration of the Eucharistic species openly signifies the bloody immolation of Christ, and is one with it.

● The new missal has also introduced the command of Christ, "Do this in memory of me" which was not previously part of the sacramental form. The memorial thus becomes the focus of attention for the new words of consecration since "the stress then is laid not on the prescription: 'Do this' but on the specification: 'Do it (*from now on* is understood) *in memory of me.*' More exactly, as Jeremias has shown these words should be translated: Do this as my memorial, and this word must be given the sense that it always has in the rabbinical literature and especially the liturgical literature of the period."[14]

Thus while the words of consecration in the traditional missal emphasize firstly transubstantiation and sacrifice, the words of the new missal exclusively emphasize the memorial and the dimension of friendship.

12. In the new missal the sacrificial offering takes place after the Consecration, and acts as a conclusion of the *anamnesis* [commemoration]. What is the nature of the sacrifice offered? Is it the sacrifice brought about during the rite by the ministry of the priest, as in the traditional missal? Is it the sacrifice which makes Christ present as Victim through the separately consecrated species of bread and wine? An examination of the texts obliges us to

---

[14]   Louis Bouyer, *op. cit.*, p.107.

draw other conclusions. In the new missal, there is a sacrificial offering in the sense that through the Eucharistic memorial which (IG §§48, 259) makes present again the historical acts of Redemption, the assembly calls to mind the sacrifice of Christ: "*Anamnesis.* In this prayer of remembrance the Church, fulfilling the command she has received from her Lord through the apostles, celebrates the memorial of Christ, calling to mind especially his blessed passion, his glorious resurrection and his ascent to heaven. *Oblation.* It is through this very memorial that the Church—in particular the Church here and now assembled—offers the immaculate Victim to God the Father, in the Holy Spirit." (IG §§55e; 55f). In this memorial offering, it is not the power of Christ's redemptive death which is presented to the Father, but rather the victorious Christ in the fulfillment of His mysteries: "Father, calling to mind the death your Son endured for our salvation, his glorious resurrection and ascension into heaven, and ready to greet him when he comes again, we offer you in thanksgiving this holy and living sacrifice" (Eucharistic Prayer III). Thus while the traditional missal brings about a sacrifice which is called "Eucharistic" in view of one of its aims, the new missal wishes to bring about a memorial of thanksgiving in which the sacrifice is one of the things commemorated.

13. The changes made to the Communion rite, though in themselves rather secondary, confirm this particular novelty of the new missal, *i.e.,* the granting of pre-eminence to the memorial meal. For example, the act of the breaking of bread has been developed largely because "…Jesus used this rite, part of a Jewish meal, when as master of the table he blessed and distributed the bread…" (CCC §1329). Hence this novelty; since brotherly sharing is an indispensable feature of the community meal, "bread used for the Eucharist, even though unleavened and of the traditional shape, ought to be made in such a way that the priest, when celebrating with a congregation, can break it into pieces and distribute these to at least some of the faithful" (IG §283). A similar observation applies to the reception of Communion. The traditional missal considers Communion as a partaking of the Victim, an act sufficiently symbolized by communicating under one species. Yet if Communion is considered primarily as a communal meal ("The celebration of the Eucharist is a paschal meal…", [IG §56]), it cannot be fully symbolized without eating *and* drinking. "The meaning of Communion is signified as clearly as possible when it is given under both kinds. In this form the meal-aspect of the Eucharist is more fully manifested" (IG §240). Similarly, since friendship and its symbolism is considered to be of primary importance, the aspect of personal sanctification represented by Communion has been relativized. At the distribution of Communion, for example, the words "May the Body and Blood of our Lord Jesus Christ keep your soul unto eternal life" have been suppressed. The serious admonitions of St. Paul[15] regarding reception of Communion, which are found in the traditional missal on Maundy Thursday and Corpus Christi, have also been suppressed in the new missal.

14. Two things are apparent from this analysis:
- The key to explaining the mystery of the Mass is no longer the Cross but the Last Supper, which has become the prime model for the rite when considered as a memorial meal. The General Instruction declares that this memorial is more than a simple commemoration in view of its power to make the mysteries of Redemption present. Moreover, the General Instruction does not deny the sacrificial dimension of the Mass, which is mentioned several times (IG §§2, 48, 54, 55, 60, 62, 153, 335, 339) without being made explicit. The General Instruction has simply brought to the foreground its memorial dimension.
- The Passion and the Resurrection are equally the object of this memorial meal (IG §2). These two mysteries are, moreover, united in a single expression; in this memorial, Christ instituted the "*Paschal* meal" (IG §56). The expression "*Paschal* sacrifice" (IG §335) is also used.

---

[15] I Cor. 11: 27-29: "Therefore whosoever shall eat this bread, or drink the chalice of the Lord unworthily, shall be guilt of the body and of the blood of the Lord."

III. Conclusion

15. One change in the liturgy particularly characterizes this new direction: the moving of the expression *Mysterium fidei*, "the mystery of faith." In the traditional missal, these words are found at the heart of the Consecration, but in the new missal they introduce the memorial acclamations after the Consecration. Their meaning is thereby changed:

- The traditional missal places the expression "*Mysterium fidei*" amid the very words of consecration in order to solicit an act of faith in the real presence of Christ brought about through transubstantiation, and also to mark the culminating point of the Mass. Here is the sacrifice; Christ is present in an immolated state wherein the species of bread and wine signify the separation of His Body and Blood during His Passion.
- In the new missal the "Mystery of Faith" is no longer the sacrificial consecration, but all the mysteries of Christ's life proclaimed and remembered together. "Let us proclaim the mystery of faith: dying you destroyed our death, rising you restored our life. Lord Jesus, come in glory. *Mysterium fidei: Mortem tuam annuntiamus, Domine, et tuam resurrectionem confitemur, donec venias.*" The second acclamation (*ad libitum*) clearly separates the *Mysterium fidei* from the Consecration and associates it with Communion: "*Quotiescumque manducamus panem hunc et calicem bibimus, mortem tuam annuntiamus, Domine, donec venias.* When we eat this bread and drink this cup, we proclaim your death, Lord Jesus, until you come in glory."

This change shifts the centre of gravity in the Mass,[16] and clearly shows the fundamental difference between the traditional missal and the new missal; in the former, the Mass is a sacrificial offering of the transubstantiated presence of Christ, while in the latter the Mass is understood as a memorial of Christ's Passover.

---

[16] *Cf.* Aimé-Georges Martimort, *Les lignes essentielles de la messe*, collection *Lex orandi*, (Paris: Cerf, 1947), p.99.

CHAPTER 2

FROM CHRIST, PRIEST AND VICTIM, TO THE LORD OF THE ASSEMBLY

16. The primacy of the memorial meal means that the missal of Paul VI, moving ever further away from the old missal, sees Christ's presence in the Mass from a new perspective. The old missal develops the sacrificial aspect of the Mass and, therefore, emphasizes the presence of Christ the Priest (in the person of the celebrant) and Christ the Victim (in the Eucharistic species). The old missal thus stands in line with the authentic teaching of the Church.[17] Since, however, the new missal is cast in the form of a memorial meal, it emphasizes the spiritual presence of Christ which is given to His faithful through His Word and His Body. The new missal shows thereby two fundamental changes: the sacramental presence of Christ the Victim is devalued, even to the point of being compared to Christ's presence in the Scriptures; moreover the *common priesthood of the faithful* becomes more important than the *ministerial priesthood of the celebrant* since it is capable of making Christ spiritually present.

I. THE SUBSTANTIAL PRESENCE OF CHRIST IN THE EUCHARISTIC SPECIES

17. The traditional missal underlines forcefully the Eucharistic presence. The numerous genuflections show the adoration due to Christ who is substantially present, Body, Blood, Soul and Divinity, in the Eucharistic species. The presence of Christ the Victim (signified by the separate consecration of the bread and wine) is considered to be the center of the liturgical action; this is the presence which is both offered to God (in the sacrificial offering) and given to men (in Communion). Such importance is not,

---

[17] Council of Trent: "For, it is one and the same Victim, the same one now offering by the ministry of the priests as He who then offered Himself on the Cross, the manner of offering alone being different" (DS 1743).

however, accorded to the presence of Christ the Victim in the new missal.

18. In the course of the liturgical action, the objective descriptions of the real presence of Christ in the host have been replaced by simplistic expressions which no longer consider the Eucharistic presence in itself but only in relation to the congregation. This is at least what many modifications suggest:

● The word *nobis*, ("for us") is systematically used whenever the Eucharistic presence is mentioned; during the presentation of the gifts (*ex quo nobis fiet panis vitae; ex quo nobis fiet potus spiritualis*), at the consecration (addition of *pro vobis tradetur*) and even in Eucharistic Prayer II, the "Canon of Hyppolitus" (*ut nobis corpus et sanguis fiant Domini nostri Jesu Christi*) though this expression is not in the original text.

● Likewise, the Eucharistic species are only designated with regard to Communion: the *hanc immaculatam hostiam* of the Offertory has become "the bread of life," the chalice is only described as *potus spiritualis* ("spiritual drink") or even, "drink of the eternal Kingdom" according to several official French translations, *etc.*

● The vocabulary of the *Institutio Generalis Missalis Romani* is significant. Neither the expression "transubstantiation" nor "Real Presence" can be found. To refer to the sacred species, the document sometimes uses the word "host" but mostly "bread." It only speaks of "the body of Christ" when directly referring to Communion. For example, §48, 3: "In the breaking of one bread the unity of the faithful is signified, and in Communion they receive the Body and Blood of the Lord as the apostles once did from the hands of Christ himself" (*cf.* §§56b, 56c, 56e, 56g, 60, *etc.*).

19. The gestures showing the respect due to the sacred species have also been reduced in number or suppressed:

● Of the 14 genuflections in the traditional missal, three alone have been kept (IG §233), and these are related to

the congregation: two are made after the people have recognized the Eucharistic presence at the elevation (the two
genuflections which immediately follow the words of consecration in the traditional missal have been suppressed)
and the third just before the distribution of Communion;
the celebrant is only required to "reverently consume the
body of Christ" (IG §116) without making a genuflection.

● The rubric which required the celebrant to keep finger and
thumb joined after the consecration out of respect for par-
ticles of the host has been suppressed. Accordingly the
purification of the fingers has also been suppressed.

● The distribution of Communion, previously restricted to
the sacred ministers, can now easily be delegated to lay
people.[18]

● The reception of Communion is marked by profane man-
ners. The communicants no longer kneel and receive on
the tongue as a sign of respect and adoration, but stand
and receive in the hand.[19]

20. In the traditional missal, the celebrant clearly identifies
the oblations with Christ the Victim by making numerous signs
of the cross over them:

● In the Offertory there are three signs of the cross over (or
with) the oblations, notably when the celebrant places
them on the corporal after the prayer of oblation. In the
new missal these gestures have disappeared from the "Preparation of the Gifts."

● Of the 26 signs of the cross over the oblations in the
Canon of the traditional missal, one alone remains in each
of the Eucharistic prayers. This is the case even for Eucharistic Prayer I which is supposed to represent the "Roman
Canon."

● In the traditional missal, the sign of the cross over the
sacred species is made again three times in the prayers

---

[18] Congregation for the Divine Worship, Instruction *Liturgicae instaurationes*,
Sept. 5, 1970, No. 6d; Code of Canon Law, Canons 230 §3; 910 §2.
[19] Congregation for Divine Worship, Instruction *Memoriale Domini*, May 29,
1969, and letter *In Reply*, DC 1544, July 20, 1969, pp.669-72.

before Communion; moreover, the celebrant makes a sign of the cross with both the host and the chalice before communicating, and does likewise as he distributes the hosts to each communicant. All these gestures have disappeared, and the sign of the cross no longer appears in the Communion rite of the new missal.

21. The prescriptions regarding sacred buildings contribute to this undermining of the real presence. By separating the tabernacle from the main altar (IG §276) the reform considers our churches less as the house of God (see Gen. 28:17 and the Introit for the Mass of the Dedication of a Church) and more as the house of the people: "The shape of the church ought in some way to suggest the form of the assembly" (IG §257). Hence the transformation of churches: "Arrangements in the nave of the church and its annexes should conform to modern requirements. Hence it is not enough to provide the immediate prerequisites for liturgical celebrations; there must also be the amenities normally found in any building wherein any considerable number of people are wont to congregate" (IG §280). Thus a Christian may enter a church where no service is in progress but far from finding himself in the presence of a Being (God in the tabernacle), he finds only an absence, *i.e.,* an absence of a liturgical action. The building only has meaning when the community is gathered together.

22. In the modifications made to the Mass, not all of which are noted here, one thing is quite clear. If the new missal recognizes the Real Presence in relation to the assembly, it never considers this presence in itself as an object of adoration. Moreover it diminishes and almost ignores the victimhood of this presence in the course of the liturgical action. All these changes—words and gestures of the new missal, the explanations in the *Institutio Generalis Missalis Romani,* the removal of the tabernacle—share the same tendency. The conception and layout of the rites of instruction ("Mass of the Catechumens") confirm this observation.

II. THE PRESENCE OF CHRIST IN HIS WORD

23. The new missal has increased the importance of the Bible as much as it has diminished the importance of the Real Presence: "When the Sacred Scriptures are read in church, God himself is speaking to his people, and Christ, present in his word, is proclaiming his Gospel" (IG §9). While indicating a new presence (Christ in his Word), this paragraph equally underlines the strict dependence of this presence on the people: "When Sacred Scripture is read *in church* (*i.e.*, before the assembly which signifies the mystery of the Church) God Himself is *speaking to His people.*" Henceforth the honor accorded to the Bible is comparable in a number of ways to the honor given to Christ's Real Presence in the Eucharistic species.

24. Scripture and the Eucharist are often described in the same way for they are ultimately two forms of that unique spiritual sustenance given to us in the Paschal banquet: both are the table of the Lord (IG §§8, 34, 56); Christ gives Himself as spiritual food (IG §§33, 56) which the assembly makes its own through a rite of Communion: "The people appropriate this divine word to themselves by their singing, and testify their fidelity to God's word by their profession of faith. Strengthened by the word of God they intercede, in the Prayer of the Faithful, for the needs of the entire Church and for the salvation of the whole world" (IG §33). These lines show the extent of this parity; a purpose similar to the Postcommunion's is attributed to the Prayers of the Faithful which have been reintroduced. The 1992 Catechism gives the same explanation:

> ...the Eucharistic table set for us is the table both of the Word of God and of the Body of the Lord. Is this not the same movement as the Paschal meal of the risen Jesus with his disciples? Walking with them he explained the Scriptures to them; sitting with them at table "he took bread, blessed and broke it, and gave it to them" (CCC §§1346, 1347).

25. The "Liturgy of the Word," considered as a meeting point between God and the congregation (IG §9), calls for a new way of looking upon Sacred Scripture, and thus compromises certain hitherto solidly established theological principles. According to the famous quotation of St. Augustine,[20] the Bible, a revealed book, actively becomes Revelation whenever it is proclaimed by the Magisterium of the Church. By virtue of the powers of order and jurisdiction, the Church's minister acts with the very authority of Christ in transmitting the deposit of Revelation: "Who hears you hears me" (Lk. 10:16). The traditional missal expresses the teaching of the Church in this matter with startling precision:

- By reserving the right of reading Sacred Scripture to ordained ministers, the missal shows the necessary action of the ecclesiastical hierarchy in the transmission of Revelation, and thus celebrates not Scripture in itself but rather its dissemination by the Magisterium of the Church. This is why the Gospel procession receives the honors usually reserved to the Real Presence.

- The traditional missal carefully sets out the Biblical readings in the context of the whole Mass. Far from being a celebration it itself, the rite is directed towards the central mystery of the Mass for which it prepares the congregation by renewing their faith. This truth is expressed perfectly at the beginning of the Canon when the celebrant prays for the faithful who are present. Addressing God, he refers to the congregation as those "...whose faith and devotion are known to Thee." These two aspects sum up the layout of the rite prior to the Offertory: from Psalm 42 to the Collect, the liturgy disposes the hearts of the faithful to fervor; from the Epistle to the Credo, the liturgy prepares the minds of the faithful by enlivening their faith. Far from being, therefore, comparable with the Eucharistic liturgy, the rite of the Gospel ought to be associated with the first prayers of the Mass (hence with them it is called the "Mass of Catechumens").

---

[20] St. Augustine, *Contra epistolam Manichaei quam vocant fundamenti*, V, 6: "I would not believe the Gospel if the authority of the Church did not compel me to—*Ego vero Evangelio non crederem, nisi me catholicae Ecclesiae commoveret auctoritas.*"

26. In the new missal, however, Sacred Scripture is celebrated in itself and no longer insofar as it is proclaimed by the hierarchy of the Church. The presence of Christ is, consequently, displaced and denatured. Christ is no longer present in His minister's teaching but directly by Himself. "When the sacred scriptures are read in church, God himself is speaking to his people, and Christ, present in his word, is proclaiming his Gospel" (IG §9). Scripture is henceforth celebrated as sufficient in itself: "…The word of God in the scripture readings is indeed addressed to all men of all times and can be understood by them…" (IG §9). It is, therefore, understandable that the role of reader can be attributed to a layperson (IG §66).

III. THE PRESENCE OF CHRIST IN THE PRIEST AND THE PEOPLE

27. The systematic weakening of the signs of the Real Presence of Christ the Victim brings in its wake the undermining of the presence of Christ the Priest "in the person of His minister"[21] and thus favors the glorification of the presence of Christ in the assembly to an extent hitherto unseen in the liturgy. The new missal undermines the distinctions between the celebrant and the faithful found in the traditional missal, and henceforth seems only to recognize one agent in the liturgy, the "People of God." The first sentence of the *Institutio Generalis Missalis Romani* describes the celebration of Mass "as an action of Christ and the people of God hierarchically ordered" (IG §1). This "liturgical assembly" (IG §323) is described in emphatic terms: it is the "holy people" (IG §§10, 62), the "people of God" (IG §§1, 7, 62, 253), "a chosen race and a royal priesthood" (IG §62), *etc.* The fact that the *Institutio Generalis Missalis Romani* mentions this notion 164 times sheds a clear light on the importance which the new missal gives to the "assembly."

A) At the Beginning of the Mass

28. The importance and dignity of the "assembly" result from its being the sign of the universal Church, which as such has

---

[21]   Pius XII, *Mediator Dei*, DS 3840.

the power to make Christ present. In focusing at length on the sacramental nature of the "assembly" (a sacrament being precisely a sign which has a certain power) the new missal underlines the importance of the spiritual presence of God in the midst of His people.

29. The symbolism of the assembly is often referred to: "This [community] represents the universal Church at a given time and place" (IG §75). This is why the Mass "wherein the bishop presides over his priests and other ministers with the people taking their full and active part" particularly merits our attention because "this is the way in which the Church is most clearly and visibly manifested" (IG §74), hence the importance of concelebration (IG §59). The opening rite of the new missal seeks to actualize this sign of the assembly: "Their [the rites'] purpose is to help the faithful who have come together in one place to make themselves into a worshipping community…" (IG §24). This notion of the assembly explains why the confession of sins becomes an act of the community and excludes the separate confession of sins by the celebrant found in the traditional missal.

30. As we have indicated, the gathering of the community is a "sacrament" with a certain power, and not merely a symbol. By "[making] themselves into a worshipping community" (IG §24) the assembly of the faithful make the Lord really present: "Then the priest, by his greeting, reminds the assembled people that the Lord is present among them. This greeting and the people's reply express the mystery of the Church formally assembled" (IG §28). From the outset, therefore, the emphasis is on the Lord's spiritual presence, and this presence will dominate the ceremony. Having devalued the presence of Christ the Victim which is brought about transubstantially through the action of the sacred minister, the new missal glorifies the spiritual presence of the Lord wrought through the ministry of the priest and people. As for the celebrant who is offering the Eucharist, he must simply "serve God and the people with dignity and humility" in order to "make the faithful realize the presence of the living Christ" (IG §60).

B) In the Liturgy of the Word

31. Once this sacramental sign of the assembly is actualized, the Liturgy of the Word takes the shape of a direct dialogue between God and His People without need for any specific action on the part of a sacred minister. We have already indicated how this rite passes over the necessary intervention of the Magisterium of the Church. Let us simply point out here how these rites are described as the joint action of the Lord and His assembled people: "When the Sacred Scriptures are read in church, God himself is speaking to his people…" (IG §9). "…God speaks to his people, reveals to them the mysteries of redemption and salvation, and provides them with spiritual nourishment; and Christ himself, in the form of his word, is present in the midst of the faithful" (IG §33). Then follows the response of the people to the action of Christ: "…The people appropriate this divine word to themselves by their singing….Strengthened by the word of God they intercede, in the Prayer of the Faithful, for the needs of the entire church and for the salvation of the whole world" (IG §33). Paragraph 45 adds that the people exercise a "priestly function" in the Prayer of the Faithful.

C) In the Liturgy of the Eucharist

32. The "Eucharistic liturgy" of the new missal patently shows how the ministerial priesthood has been pushed aside in favor of the communal action of the assembly. The sacrificial offering is only seen through the prism of the common priesthood of the faithful, a novelty which threatens equally the character of the ministerial priesthood and the sacramental power of the sacrifice. The Church has always distinguished the unbloody immolation brought about by the consecration, from the sacrificial offering (oblation in this limited sense[22]) made by the participants through which they unite themselves to the sacramental oblation accomplished by Christ the Priest in the person of His minister. Only the unbloody immolation at the consecration, "performed by the priest and by him alone, as the representative of Christ and not as the representative of the faithful,"[23] belongs to the category

---

[22] Pius XII, *Mediator Dei,* DS 3852.
[23] Pius XII, *Mediator Dei*, DS 3852.

of sacrament: the action of Christ works *ex opere operato* [in virtue of the action performed]. On the other hand, the oblation in the restricted sense of the word works *ex opere operantis* [in virtue of the one performing the actions]: the participation of the faithful consists in their uniting themselves "by virtue of their intention"[24] to the sacramental offering that Christ the Priest makes of Himself to His Father in the person of His minister. The new missal omits this distinction and ignores systematically the specifically sacramental action of the minister who alone acts by virtue of Christ the Priest.

33. Thus each time the *Institutio Generalis Missalis Romani* considers the offering of the sacrifice, it describes it as an act both of the celebrant and of the faithful. Take for example §54: "The meaning of the prayer is that all the faithful now gathered together unite themselves with Christ in praising the wonderful works of God and in offering sacrifice." Once again the two actors of the liturgical celebration are seen to be Christ and the Assembly. This emphasis on the assembly is confirmed again in the following paragraph: "*Oblation.* It is through this very memorial that the Church—in particular the Church here and now assembled—offers the immaculate Victim to God the Father, in the Holy Spirit. The Church strives also that the faithful should not only offer the immaculate victim but should learn to offer themselves..." (IG §55*ff*). This offering is the work of the common priesthood: "The faithful constitute...a royal priesthood...that they may give thanks to God and offer the immaculate Victim, not only through the hands of the priest but also with him..." (IG §62).

34. The prayers of the traditional missal expressing the sacramental oblation, which is alone offered by the sacred minister, have thus been suppressed in the new missal. The first prayer of the Offertory in the traditional missal, composed quite deliberately in the first person singular, shows this ritual oblation: "Accept, O holy Father,...this unspotted host which I, Thy unworthy servant, offer unto Thee, my living and true God...." The offering of the chalice, however, indicates the participation of the as-

---

[24]   *Ibid.*

sembly in the offering (taken in its restricted sense): "We offer unto Thee, O Lord, the chalice of salvation." In the new missal, on the contrary, the prayers of the Offertory (or rather the "Presentation of the Gifts") are systematically in the first person plural. If the *Orate fratres* ("Brethren, pray that my sacrifice and yours may be acceptable to God the Father almighty") has been kept *in extremis*,[25] a number of official translations [in the French] have knowingly suppressed the distinction between the types of offering[26]: "At the moment of offering the sacrifice of the entire Church, let us pray together." Henceforth the offering belongs no longer to the celebrant but to the assembled people. An expression used in Eucharistic Prayer III illustrates this change: "*Populum tibi congregare non desinis, ut a solis ortu usque ad occasum oblatio munda offeratur nomini tuo.*"[27]

35. The ministerial priesthood of the celebrant is never once mentioned as the unique cause of the real presence of Christ under the species of bread and wine (and thus cause of the sacramental offering). Only his role as president of the assembly, whereby the people offer the sacrifice "by the hands of the priest," is explained at any length:

● The priest's role as president of the assembly is mentioned 13 times in the *Institutio Generalis Missalis Romani* and dominates the entire liturgical ceremony, since, with the

---

[25] Annibale Bugnini, *La riforma liturgica*, Edizioni liturgiche (Rome, 1983), p.352 (especially Note 19) and p.374.

[26] One of the members of the commission for Francophone liturgical translations wrote that even if "the reformers of the missal avoided expressions which might contain such an ambiguity, nevertheless certain traditional expressions should be minimized in the translation [of the Offertory] in the light of what we have said concerning the true character of this opening up of the Eucharistic Liturgy" (Antoine Dumas, "*Pour mieux comprendre les textes liturgiques du missel traditionnel*," *Notitiae* 54, May 1970, p.199. Dumas was a member of the *Consilium* and of the Congregation for Divine Worship).

[27] Literally, "You cease not to gather your people together *in order that* from the rising of the sun to its setting, a pure oblation might be offered to your Name." The official French translation has further worsened this expression by turning from the passive to the active voice: "You cease not to gather your people together so that they might everywhere offer to you a pure offering."

exception of one or two prayers by way of personal preparation, all the celebrant's prayers are of the nature of one
presiding (IG §13).

- In the two instances (IG §§10, 60) where the celebrant is
  said to take the place of Christ, he does so representing
  Christ the Head: "It is his function therefore to *preside over
  the community*; it is for him to lead their prayer, to proclaim to them the good news of salvation and to *associate
  the people with himself in offering the sacrifice....*" If the cor-
  rection of 1970 added that the priest has the power to offer
  sacrifice "in the person of Christ," this expression follows
  the statement that the priest belongs to "the community of
  the faithful" over whom he presides: "In virtue of his ordi-
  nation, the priest is the member of the community who
  possesses the power to offer the sacrifice in the person of
  Christ. It is his function, therefore, to preside over the
  community; it is for him to lead their prayer, to proclaim
  to them the good news of salvation and to associate the
  people with himself in offering the sacrifice to God...."
  This passage, therefore, should seemingly be interpreted as
  referring to the presidential offering by which the priest
  takes the place of Christ the Head, and not to the sacramental offering by which the priest takes the place of
  Christ the unique High Priest.
- The Catechism of 1992 (§1348) confirms this: "...it is he
  himself [Christ] who presides invisibly over every Eucharistic celebration. It is in representing him that the bishop
  or priest acting *in the person of Christ the head (in persona
  Christi capitis)* presides over the assembly, speaks after the
  readings, receives the offerings, and says the Eucharistic
  Prayer."

Thus the priest is only described in the context of his relation
to the people of God and not in terms of the power he alone possesses to consecrate *in persona Christi* the real Body of Christ and
make the sacrificial offering. The presence of Christ the Priest (in
His minister) has thus been undermined or even erased from the
new missal in favor of the People of God who are looked upon as
the cause of Christ's spiritual presence in their midst.

IV. CONCLUSION

36. While the traditional missal emphasizes the presence of Christ in the priest *per virtutem* [through the power he has received] before elaborating the devotion due to the host after the Consecration, the new missal focuses rather upon the spiritual presence of the Lord brought about at the start of Mass by virtue of the coming together of the community. The Mass is thus considered as an action both of Christ and of the assembly (IG §1). The spiritual presence of the Lord is made tangible as "Word" in the Liturgy of the Word (IG §9), and then as an oblation in the memorial of His acts which are made present once again (IG §1). At the same time the people are fed at the table of the God's Word, and at the table of the Christ's Body (IG §8). One sees, therefore, that the liturgical reform has undermined the sacramental presence of Christ the Victim while exalting His presence in Scripture; only thus is manifested the intended likeness between these two ways in which Christ gives Himself as "spiritual food" (IG §§33, 56).

37. Henceforth the Mass is, therefore, a memorial meal at which the Lord is made present by the coming together of His people. Such is the result of this analysis, and the first version of the *Institutio Generalis Missalis Romani* declared as much in §7:

● In the Mass or Lord's Supper the People of God are called together into one place where the priest presides over them. They assemble to celebrate the Memorial of the Lord. Hence the promise of Christ: "Wherever two or three are gathered together in my name, there am I in the midst of them." [Latin text (1969 version): *Cena dominica sive missa est sacra synaxis seu congregatio populi Dei in unum convenientis, sacerdote praeside, ad memoriale Domini celebrandum. Quare de sanctae Ecclesiae locali congregatione eminenter valet promissio Christi: "Ubi sunt duo vel tres congregati in nomine meo, ibi sum in medio eorum"* (Mt. 18:20).]

This description of the Mass which mentioned neither its sacrificial nature nor the substantial presence of Christ in the Eucharistic species provoked forceful reactions. The version of 1970 returned to certain traditional expressions:

● In the Mass or Lord's Supper the People of God are called together into one place where the priest presides over them and acts in the person of Christ. They assemble to celebrate the Memorial of the Lord, which is the sacrifice of the Eucharist. Hence the promise of Christ: "Wherever two or three are gathered together in my name, there am I in the midst of them" applies in a special way to this gathering of the local church. For in the celebration of the Mass whereby the sacrifice of the Cross is perpetuated, Christ is really present in the very community which has gathered in His name in the person of His minister and also substantially and continuously under the eucharistic species. [Latin text (1970 version): *In Missa seu Cena dominica populus Dei in unum convocatur, sacerdote praeside personamque Christi gerente ad memoriale Domini seu sacrificium eucharisticum celebrandum. Quare de huiusmodi sanctae Ecclesiae coadunatione locali eminenter valet promissio Christi: "Ubi sunt duo vel tres congregati in nomine meo, ibi sum in medio eorum." In Missae enim celebratione, in qua sacrificium Crucis perpetuatur, Christus realiter praesens adest in ipso coetu in suo nomine congregato, in persona ministri, in verbo suo, et quidem substantialiter et continenter sub speciebus eucharisticis.*]

These substantial additions brought about no rectification of the rite itself. Moreover, they pass over the novelty introduced by the version of 1969. Although the priest is said to act *in persona Christi* and that the Mass is a sacrifice, these traditional expressions are subject to a new interpretation according to their context: the priest represents the person of Christ the Head *insofar as he presides over the assembly,* and the Mass is a sacrifice because it is the *memorial* meal of the Cross. Thus the essential idea remains undisturbed; the spiritual presence of Christ in the midst of His people takes center stage.

CHAPTER 3

FROM PROPITIATION
TO THANKSGIVING

38. In the last chapter, we pointed out that the new missal grants the human participants in the liturgy a dignity and importance which they did not have in the traditional missal. Whereas the traditional missal led the celebrant to consider himself an "unworthy servant" (*Suscipe sancte Pater*), the new missal gives him this prayer to say: "We offer you, Father, this life-giving bread, this saving cup. We thank you for counting us worthy to stand in your presence and serve you" (Eucharistic Prayer II). This change in perspective corresponds in fact to a new way of considering sin, which in itself is related to the Mass in two ways; if sin can be an obstacle to the approval of the offering (Mt. 5:24), this same sacrifice accepted by God is the very antidote to sin (Heb. 9:28).

● Though the new missal recognizes man's need to be converted, it supposes a state of total peace with God at the beginning of the rite: once man has repented there is no obstacle to the offering either on God's side or on man's. In contrast, the traditional missal calls to mind the fact that insofar as the punishment due for sin has not been remitted, unworthy man still finds himself somewhat in conflict with the God he has offended. Thus relying on the intercession of Christ and the merits of the saints, he prays that in spite of his unworthiness, God may accept his offering.

● Regarding the fruits of the Mass, the new missal certainly asks for the divinization brought by Jesus Christ, the antidote to future sin, but it never concerns itself with the punishment due for past sins: in its prayers the new missal never asks for the application of that infinite satisfaction for sin made by Christ.

Thus the issue of punishment due for sin is no longer a subject for prayer: the offering is presented to God as if the traces of past sins posed no obstacle to God's approval, and the fruits of the Mass regarding satisfaction for sin are passed over in silence. Moreover, sorrow for sin is itself greatly diminished. Let us analyze these points.

I. THE OFFERING AND SORROW FOR SIN

39. In the traditional missal, prayers of compunction for sin return again and again, even at the solemn moment of the Preface; they are, as it were, the breathing of the soul. Having acknowledged his sins (*Confiteor*) man prays that his sins may be forgiven (*Oramus te*), and asks that his heart and lips may be purified (*Munda cor meum*). Coming before God with a humble and contrite heart (*In spiritu humilitatis*), he asks for His mercy (*Incensum istud*); he strongly protests that he is not of that number who wish to live in sin (*Lavabo*). This elaboration of the various elements of contrition shows the full extent of the prayer offered by the celebrant as he ascends the altar steps: "Take away from us our iniquities, we beseech Thee, O Lord, that we may be worthy to enter with pure minds into the Holy of Holies, through Christ our Lord" (*Aufer a nobis*). If, on the contrary, the new missal contains certain penitential elements, these are unusually brief and deficient. Only in the shortened penitential rite at the start of Mass do the faithful express their sorrow for sin. The dispositions of the celebrant are renewed by a few short prayers said in a low voice "in his personal capacity" (IG §13): the *Per evangelica dicta*, the *In spiritu humilitatis* and the short verse *Lava me*, which replaces Psalm 25. This impoverishment of the rite which contrasts with the graceful precision of the prayers in the traditional missal has been made worse still by translations. For example, the *In spiritu humilitatis et in animo contrito* has been rendered in the new French missal as "*Humbles et pauvres*" (humble and poor); the element of contrition has thus disappeared.

40. A soul whose sins are forgiven is not thereby fully approved of by God; insofar as one has failed to satisfy the demands of justice by bearing the punishment due to sin, one remains partially unjustified and thus unworthy to offer unaided an acceptable sacrifice. From the beginning of the Mass, the traditional missal emphasizes this unworthiness by the position of the sacred minister in the sanctuary: not at the altar but at the foot of the altar, *a longe*. Like the publican, he keeps his eyes downcast and strikes his breast (Lk. 18:13). This unworthiness of the minister of the sacrifice means that God's acceptance of the sacrifice is considered as an unmerited grace, a grace asked for in reverential fear: "Accept, O holy Father,…this unspotted host, which I, Thy unworthy servant, offer unto Thee" (*Suscipe sante Pater*). The Church addresses God in this way more than ten times during the course of the Offertory and the Canon. Now these requests for approval no longer form a constituent part of the new missal: they are found neither in the preparation of the gifts, nor in Eucharistic Prayer II. Only Eucharistic Prayers III and IV use once the term "*respice*" ("look") and then only after the consecration.

41. In view of the deficiency of the minister, the traditional missal places between the celebrant and God a principal mediator, Jesus Christ, and subordinate mediators, the saints. The sacrificial offering depends firstly on the intercession of Christ, present throughout the liturgical action. This intercession is sought at the very opening of the Canon: "We therefore humbly pray and beseech Thee, most merciful Father, through Jesus Christ, Thy Son, our Lord, that thou wouldst vouchsafe to accept and bless these gifts" (*Te igitur*). According to a common interpretation,[28] Christ's intercession is again invoked in the solemn prayer of offering following the consecration (*Supplice te rogamus*): "We must humbly beseech Thee, almighty God, command these offerings to be borne by the hands of Thy holy Angels to Thine altar on high, in the sight of Thy divine Majesty." Above all, this intercession is inscribed in the very framework of the Canon: the prayers surrounding the words of consecration all finish with the words: "Through Christ our Lord." Now the new missal has almost suppressed all mention of the mediation of Christ in the offering of the sacrifice. The first two examples mentioned above are no longer found in the new Eucharistic Prayers. The expression "Through Christ our Lord," which is now optional in Eucharistic Prayer I, has been suppressed in the other Eucharistic Prayers. It

---

28   Pierre le Brun, *op. cit.*, p.463.

only appears at the end to introduce the *Per ipsum* and looks forward to the heavenly liturgy: "...make us worthy to share eternal life with Mary, the virgin mother of God, with the apostles, and with all the saints who have done your will throughout the ages. May we praise you in union with them, and give you glory through your Son, Jesus Christ." (Eucharistic Prayer II); "Welcome into your kingdom our departed brothers and sisters, and all who have left this world in your friendship. We hope to enjoy for ever the vision of your glory, through Christ our Lord, from whom all good things come." (Eucharistic Prayer III); "Father, in your mercy grant also to us, your children, to enter into our heavenly inheritance....Then, in your kingdom, freed from the corruption of sin and death, we shall sing your glory with every creature through Christ our Lord, through whom you give us everything that is good" (Eucharistic Prayer IV).

42. The traditional missal again calls upon the intercession and merits of the saints. Having confessed our sins before the saints (*Confiteor*), we rely upon their merits to obtain for us the divine pardon (*Oramus te*). Through the intercession of St. Michael and of all the saints (*Per intercessionem*), incense is offered with a sweet savor to God. The most Holy Virgin, St. John the Baptist and Saints Peter and Paul intercede for us (*Suscipe sancta Trinitas*) and we ask for strength and divine protection while emphasizing their merits (*Communicantes*). Now, the new missal has abandoned this dimension of the rite. The invocations mentioned have not been used in any of the new prayers. Eucharistic Prayer III alone once mentions the intercession of the saints, but in none of the prayers are their merits called upon. When the saints are mentioned, it is exclusively in view of the union that we will enjoy with them when God opens heaven to us. The prayers of the Proper of the Saints have suffered a similar fate since the new missal has suppressed most of the 200 prayers[29] in which the traditional missal invoked the saints' merits. Only three obligatory prayers make mention of them in the entire liturgical year.

---

[29] *Cf.* Placide Bruylants, *Les oraisons du missel romain* (Mont-César, 1952), Vol. I *index verborum.* [Bruylants was a member of the *Consilium.*]

II. The Satisfaction Due for Sin

43. In diminishing the importance of the intercession of Christ and our dependence on the merits of the saints, and moreover, by no longer mentioning the unworthiness of the liturgy's human agents, the new missal gives the impression that the consequences of sin are no obstacle to the approval of the sacrifice. This disregard of the punishment due for sin, and hence of divine justice, is also apparent when one analyses the fruits now expected from the Mass. To obtain the remission of punishments due for the sins of the living and the dead, the traditional missal calls upon the merits of the Passion of Christ, and those of the saints which complement it (Col. 1:24). The living are also thereby taught to conform themselves to the Passion of Christ. These nuances, however, are almost entirely absent from the new missal.

44. The changes made to the Collects of the Mass throughout the liturgical year are revealing. Henceforth the prayers only ask that we be "purified from the stains of sin": this request, frequently made in the traditional missal (ten times in the Proper of the Saints for August alone), now appears in only a few ferial Masses of Lent. If the traditional missal made us honor St. Raymond de Penafort (Jan. 23) as "wonderful minister of the sacrament of Penance" in order to ask the grace to "bring forth worthy fruits of penance," the Collect of the new missal leaves both these aspects aside and speaks only of his love for sinners. The new missal has also ceased to recommend meditation on the Passion of Christ (St. Paul of the Cross, April 28), to recall that the Servites (Feb. 12) were devoted to the sorrows of our Lady, to emphasize that St. Luke (Oct. 18) "bore ever in his body the mortification of the Cross," *etc.* The scriptural readings in the new missal are subject to the same process, *i.e.,* the reduction of all references to divine justice. We have noted above how I Cor. 11: 27 has been suppressed in Eucharistic epistles, but there are more examples besides; the Gospel of the 12th Sunday in Ordinary Time, Year A, omits Mt. 10:28: "And fear ye not them that kill the body and are not able to kill the soul: but rather fear him that can destroy both soul and body in hell"; the second reading of the 20th Sunday in Ordinary Time, Year A, leaves out Rom. 11:19-23 where St. Paul reminds us that our unfaithfulness can bring upon us the punishment that struck Israel, *etc.*

45. The liturgy for the deceased equally fails to mention the punishment due for sin. This appears in the *Institutio Generalis Missalis Romani:* "The Church offers the Paschal Sacrifice for the Dead so that, through the union of all with each other in Christ, the dead may be helped by prayers and the living may be consoled by hope" (IG §335). Where we could have expected the expression "propitiatory sacrifice for the remission of punishment," we only find "Paschal sacrifice" (the expression is used again in IG §339) so that the dead might be "helped by prayers."

● Likewise, the *Ordo Missae* of the new missal completely draws a veil over the sufferings of the souls in purgatory. In asking for a *locum refrigerii* for the faithful departed, the traditional missal clearly shows the punishments that the deceased might be suffering. The new prayers simply say "Receive them into your Kingdom" (Eucharistic Prayer III) or "…bring them and all the departed into the light of your presence" (Eucharistic Prayer II). Eucharistic Prayer IV goes further by asking nothing for the souls of the departed, referring them to God merely by the word "Remember."

● The same observation must be made when we compare the Requiem Masses of the two missals. In the prayers of the proper, the traditional missal underlines clearly the propitiatory value of the sacrifice, and asks that the dead may be released from their sins. The new missal, however, emphasizes the happiness of heaven and the resurrection. The Tract, the *Dies Irae*, and the Offertory antiphon, which all focused on propitiation, have been suppressed in the new missal.

III. CONCLUSION

46. Everything even remotely associated with the punishment due to sin—from the liturgy of the dead to the Ordinary of the Mass, from the prayers of the Proper to the scriptural read-

ings—has been diminished or even suppressed by the liturgical reform. Thus the propitiatory dimension has, as it were, disappeared from the new missal. This fact is merely the logical conclusion of what we previously established; if the Mass is considered firstly as a memorial rather than a sacrifice, if the presence of Christ the Priest fades into a general presence of Christ and His mysteries, it is clear that the propitiatory aim of the sacrifice, so firmly reiterated by the Council of Trent, could only be abandoned in favor of prayers of thanksgiving. A reading of the *Institutio Generalis Missalis Romani* leaves no doubt in this matter; the propitiatory dimension is never mentioned while the Eucharistic aim appears frequently (§§2, 7, 48, 54, 55, 62, 259, 335, 339). A new vocabulary has been forged around this modernization of values; the expressions "Eucharistic celebration" (§§4, 5, 6, 24, 43, 48, 56, 59, 60, 66, 101, 253, 260, 280, 282, 283, 284), "Eucharistic liturgy," and "Mass," on the other hand, is used considerably less,[30] not to mention the expression "Sacrifice of the Mass," which has become obsolete.

47. A new understanding of the Mass then appears; it is less an application of the merits of Redemption and more a liturgy of the saved—the liturgy of a "people your Son has gained for you (*populus acquisitionis tuae*)" (Eucharistic Prayer III). Rather than being an action whereby the priest *in persona Christi* applies the merits and satisfactions won by Christ in His redemptive sacrifice, the Mass is the action of a people—"the sacred assembly, a chosen race, a royal priesthood" (IG §62)—who celebrate with thanksgiving a Redemption already released in full (IG §54).

---

[30] *Cf.* L. M. Renier, *Exultet, encyclopédie pratique de la liturgie* (CNPL, 2000), p.136.

PART TWO

THE PRINCIPLE BEHIND THE LITURGICAL REFORM

THE PASCHAL MYSTERY

Thesis

48. In Part One, our analysis enabled us to note the numerous, substantial differences between the traditional missal and the new missal. At this point in our study, we must highlight the unifying principle behind these reforms in order to appreciate their importance fully. The key to interpreting the reforms appeared in official documents as early as 1964: it is the *Paschal mystery*. The Declaration *Inter Oecumenici* states in fact that:

> First of all, however, it is essential that everybody be persuaded that the scope of the Constitution on the Sacred Liturgy is not limited merely to the changing of liturgical rites and texts. Rather its aim is to foster the formation of the faithful and that pastoral activity of which the liturgy is the summit and the source (see Const. Art. 10). The changes in the liturgy which have already been introduced, or which will be introduced later, have this same end in view. The thrust of pastoral activity which is centered on the liturgy is to give expression to the Paschal Mystery in people's lives.[31]

On the 25th anniversary of the Constitution *Sacrosanctum Concilium*, Pope John Paul II spoke about the main ideas which led to the liturgical reform, and reminded the Church of the importance of the Paschal mystery: "The first principle is the 'actualization' of the Paschal mystery of Christ in the Church's liturgy."[32] Our study of the Paschal mystery is a response to Pope John Paul's desire that theologians should explore "points of doctrine which, perhaps because they are new, have not been well understood by

---

[31] *Inter Oecumenici*, Sept. 26, 1964, Nos. 5 and 6.
[32] John Paul II, *Vicesimus Quintus Annus*, December 4, 1988, DC 1985, June 4, 1989, p.519.

some sections of the Church."[33] In this second part we will seek to show the theological principles at the heart of the liturgical reform, and in Part Three we will evaluate these doctrinal innovations.

49. The "Paschal mystery" is above all a new way of looking at the Redemption. Since the Mass is the continuation of Christ's redemptive work, the liturgical reform will trace its source back to the Redemption: whatever distinguishes the Paschal mystery from the Redemption—the change of name corresponds to a radical change of ideas—will distinguish the new missal from the traditional missal (Chapter 1). The notion of Paschal mystery includes, nevertheless, man's participation in the Redemption through the sacraments; does not the Greek term *mysterion* also translate as "sacrament"? This "theology of mysteries" must, therefore, be analyzed (Chapter 2). Lastly, we will examine how the memorial rite forms the link between the new theology of Redemption and the theology of mysteries (Chapter 3). The three sections of Part Two will enable us to understand and justify the three observations previously made:

- The new theology explains the diminution, not to say suppression, of propitiation in the new missal (Part One, Chapter 3)
- The theology of mysteries accounts for the innovations regarding the notion of presence in the Mass (Part One, Chapter 2).
- An understanding of the sense which this new theology gives to the word "memorial" explains the abandoning of the sacrificial rite in favor of a memorial meal (Part One, Chapter 1).

50. In the three chapters that follow we will bring together the theses of the new theology, looking at the writings of those theologians responsible for the liturgical reform and at official post-conciliar texts. Our exposé could have been amply illustrated from either source, but using both will lend weight to our analy-

---

[33] John Paul II, *Ecclesia Dei Afflicta*, July 2, 1988.

sis, and show how the new missal is the practical application of the new theology. The historical role of Vatican II will be dealt with in special sections throughout the analysis. By adopting the new theology the Council called for the liturgical reform and made it possible. If the new missal is the missal of the new theology, history shows that it is also the missal of the Council. We will, moreover, quote from the 1992 Catechism, not so much to prove our theses as to show how the general tenor of this important document confirms the results of our analysis.

CHAPTER 1

THE PASSOVER
OF THE LORD

"The Paschal Mystery is Christ at the summit of the revelation of the inscrutable mystery of God."—Pope John Paul II, *Dives in Misericordia* (§9).

51. The expression "Paschal mystery" appears only a few times in the writings of the Church Fathers. In the ancient sacramentaries it appears more frequently but is used in the plural. In the Gelasian sacramentary, it is used once in the singular in the Collect of Monday in Holy Week (which later became the third Postcommunion prayer on Good Friday in the *Ordo Hebdomodae Sanctae Instauratus* of 1956). Until the 20th century the expression had no special meaning in the writings of theologians. Today, however,

> the Paschal mystery has become the foundation of, and the key to, the meaning of the entire Christian liturgy....The Paschal mystery expands the boundaries of the liturgy making it the basis and inspiration of the moral life, of all the decisions of the believer and, as it were, of all Christian spirituality. [34]

Is this Paschal mystery a total innovation? Not according to the new theology. It is a fresh look at the traditional dogma of the Redemption: "What we call Paschal mystery, classic theology called the dogma of the Redemption. It is easy to see how Redemption and Paschal mystery coincide broadly speaking." [35]

52. The first reason given for abandoning the expression "Redemption" is that it is considered too negative. By developing the notion of objective Redemption, classic theology is thought to have overemphasized the satisfaction of justice, the cooperation of

---

[34] Pietri Sorci, article "*Mistero pasquale*," NDL, p.824.
[35] Aimon-Marie Roguet, "*Qu'est-ce que le mystère pascal?*" LMD 67, 3rd Trimester 1961, p.9. [Roguet was a member of the *Consilium*.]

man and the pains of Christ's Passion. The Paschal mystery will seemingly put things back into their proper perspective by emphasizing the great importance of love, the initiative of God, and the new life of the Resurrection:

> Redemption takes the form of a problem to be solved....How can an infinite offense be atoned for? How can one person make up for all? How can somebody who is innocent pay for somebody who is guilty? It is unfortunate that these are the terms in which Redemption is presented to many of our contemporaries. Some are scandalized in their sense of justice, and think that such a Redemption is an unanswerable objection to the goodness of God. If God were truly Father, would He be so exacting in His accounts, and would He take out His anger on His beloved Son? In the theology of the Paschal mystery, one does not meet with such pitfalls. Our salvation now appears to be wrought by a vital, free, and purely voluntary initiative coming entirely from God's merciful love.[36]

The theology of the Paschal mystery implies, therefore, the abandoning of a former position, because it no longer wishes to consider the Passion of Christ as a propitiatory offering to divine justice offended by sin. Justifying this change demands a new theology of sin in which the work of Redemption appears in a new light: disregarding justice, it is now the work of love, whereby God reveals the infinite charity with which He pursues man, even when man sins. The humanity of Christ need no longer offer satisfaction to appease the divine anger provoked by our offences.

I. THE NEW THEOLOGY

(A) A New Theology of Sin

53. According to many contemporary theologians, sin must not be looked upon from the perspective of the divine anger, since it incurs no debt in justice with regard to God. They say that just as God gains nothing from the gifts His creatures give to Him, so He loses nothing through sin:

> It is unquestionably a great truth that sin has something infinite about it since firstly it destroys in man a reality of infinite

---

[36] Aimon-Marie Roguet, *op. cit.*, pp.10-11.

value, *i.e.,* the life of grace, and also because escaping the slavery of sin is an act beyond all human powers. Sin is not, however, prejudicial to God. In the same way that Creation and God's giving of life to man add nothing to God Himself, so sin takes nothing away from Him. [37]

Such a statement is considerably ambiguous; while it is obvious that sin takes nothing away from God's *nature*, it prejudices, nevertheless, His right to be adored and obeyed. The same confusion appears in the writings of many authors:

> The notion of sin is equivocal. It seems to be an injury against God, in which case reparation would be eminently fitting. Sin is, however, not prejudicial at all to the nature of God which is inaccessible; the only thing it harms is the nature of man. [38]

What is again forgotten in this example is that one can offend the honor of God (and so owe reparation) without touching His nature. In classic theology, sin is an offense against the honor of God, and is measured by the scale of the infinite majesty of the person offended rather than by the harm the sinner does to himself. God has in fact created all things for His own glory, and man must direct all of his actions to that end: "Whether you eat or drink, or whatsoever else you do, do all to the glory of God" (I Cor. 10:31). By refusing to give due honor to God, the sinner makes himself God's enemy and incurs a debt against His justice. According to the new theology, however, man's sin seems to harm only himself and society without being prejudicial to God. Moreover, sin does not offend the justice of God, but offends only His love insofar as it constitutes a refusal of this love. The same view emerges from the 1992 Catechism:

> Sin is an offense against reason, truth, and right conscience; it is failure in genuine love for God and neighbor caused by a perverse attachment to certain goods. It wounds the nature of man and injures human solidarity. Sin is an offense against God (Ps. 51:6). Sin sets itself against God's love for us and turns our hearts away from it (CCC §§1849, 1850).

---

[37] Yves de Montcheuil, *Leçons sur le Christ*, (Paris: Editions de l'Epi, 1949), pp.126-29.

[38] Adalbert Hamman, *La Rédemption et l'Histoire du monde* (Paris: Alsatia, 1947), pp.63, 67, 71-72. [Hamman was a member of the *Consilium*.]

54. Intent on glorifying the liberality of God in the work of Creation, the new theology believes that to make God into a jealous defender of His own honor would be to obscure this liberality. It maintains that God's love for us never lessens, even when our hearts would be closed to it:

> God loves his people more than a bridegroom his beloved; his love will be victorious over even the worst infidelities and will extend to his most precious gift: "God so loved the world that he gave his only Son" (Jn. 3:16). God's love is "everlasting": "For the mountains may depart and the hills be removed, but my steadfast love shall not depart from you" (Is. 54:10). Through Jeremiah, God declares to his people, "I have loved you with an everlasting love; therefore I have continued my faithfulness to you" (Jer. 31:3) (CCC §§219, 220).

Since God's love endures in spite of sin, and since His justice demands no satisfaction, it would be contrary to God's goodness to punish us for our faults. The unhappiness that comes from sin, therefore, comes only from man himself or from creation, but not from God. This position, however, leads to the neglect of Saint Paul's teaching that sin provokes God's anger,[39] an anger represented on earth[40] by the imposition of punishment[41] and which will break forth especially at the Last Judgment.[42] The 1992 Catechism is marked by the "neglect" of this teaching. If it speaks of hell, it considers it only as self-exclusion from the love of God (CCC §1033) and never as a punishment that God inflicts on man, the obstinate sinner.

55. Consequently, the need to satisfy divine justice is no longer apparent, and the doctrine of the vicarious satisfaction of Christ[43] appears scandalous:

> Second enigma and second scandal: not only has the Eternal Father chosen His own Son to make expiation in our place, but faced with the most innocent and beloved of victims, the victim

---

[39] Rom. 6:15 and 9:22; Col. 3:6; Eph. 2:3,5,6.
[40] Rom. 1:18*ff*.; I Thess. 2:16.
[41] Heb. 3:9-11.
[42] Rom. 2:5*ff*., 3:5,12:19; I Thess. 1:10, 5:9; Heb. 4:3.
[43] Rom. 5:9: "Christ died for us; much more therefore, being now justified by his blood, shall we be saved from wrath through him."

most capable of moving God in His compassion, He asks him for compensation of the most humiliating and painful kind! ...What harshness! What incomprehensible insensitivity! Let us say rather, gentlemen: what an abominable way to interpret the thoughts of God! Nothing justifies it in the least.[44]

If the word "satisfaction" is occasionally kept, it is only on the grounds that it is "not a demand of God's love, but what love requires in us."[45] This "satisfaction" becomes identified with the recovery of our own *spiritual health* and especially of our capacity to love:

> But sin also injures and weakens the sinner himself, as well as his relationships with God and neighbor. Absolution takes away sin, but it does not remedy all the disorders sin has caused. Raised up from sin, the sinner must still recover his full spiritual health by doing something more to make amends for the sin: he must "make satisfaction for" or "expiate" his sins (CCC §1459).

One thing is clear; satisfaction is described from now on as a purely corrective punishment and no longer at all in terms of God's vengeance.

(B) A New Theology of Redemption

56. The popes prior to Vatican II have often summarized the classic doctrine of the Redemption in their encyclicals. Redemption is described as a work of love, but of a love which appeases the divine justice:

> The mystery of the Divine Redemption is firstly and by its nature a mystery of love; the mystery of Christ's love of justice towards His heavenly Father, to whom the sacrifice of the Cross is offered in a spirit of loving obedience, gives the superabundant and infinite satisfaction which the sins of the human race made necessary; "By suffering out of love and obedience, Christ gave more to God than was required to compensate for the offense of the whole human race" (*ST*, III, Q. 48, A. 2). Moreover, it is the mystery of the merciful love of the august Trinity and of the Divine Redeemer towards men. We were in fact totally incapable of making proper expiation for our sins. Christ, however,

---

[44] Henry Pinard de la Boullaye, Conférences de Notre Dame de Paris, *Jésus Rédempteur* (Spes, 1936), pp.119-20.

[45] Yves Montcheuil, *op. cit.*, pp.133-34.

through the unfathomable riches of His merits, borne of the shedding of His precious blood, was able to re-establish and conclude the pact of friendship between God and men, that pact which was first violated in Eden by Adam's sin and later on by the innumerable sins of the chosen people. Moved by His ardent charity for us and acting as our rightful and perfect Mediator, the Divine Redeemer has completely harmonized the duty and obligations of humanity with the rights of God. He is thus the true author of that marvellous reconciliation between divine justice and divine mercy where lies the absolute transcendence of our salvation.[46]

57. From the perspective of the Paschal mystery, the Redemption, which "is not meant to give something back to God, but to give God back to man,"[47] is seen quite differently. Redemption is no longer the satisfaction of divine justice as wrought by Christ, but rather the supreme *revelation* of the eternal Covenant which God has made with humanity, and which has never been destroyed by sin.

> It is precisely beside the path of man's eternal election to the dignity of being an adopted child of God that there stands in history the cross of Christ, the only-begotten Son, who, as "light from light, true God from true God," came to give the final witness to the wonderful covenant of God with humanity, of God with man—every human being.[48]

The Redemption then reveals to us "the depth of that love which does not recoil before the extraordinary sacrifice of the Son, in order to satisfy the fidelity of the Creator and Father towards human beings...."[49] The word "satisfy" as it is used here loses its particular theological connotation. It is not a matter of satisfying for an offense against justice, but rather of "responding" to God's fidelity towards man. In Christ's response to this fidelity,

---

[46]   Pius XII, *Haurietis Aquas*, May 15, 1956, AAS 48 (1956). Translation from the Daughters of St. Paul edition.

[47]   Emile Mersch, *Théologie du Corps mystique* (Paris: Desclée de Bouwer, 1949), Vol. I, p.329. *Cf.* Louis Richard, *Le Mystère de la Redemption* (Desclée, 1959), pp.146, 213, 243*ff.*

[48]   John Paul II, *Dives in Misericordia*, November 30, 1980, No. 7.

[49]   John Paul II, *ibid.*

man discovers the unchanged love of the Father which is stronger than all the obstacles which man puts in its way:

> If God has sent His Son to open again the gates of salvation to all men, it is because His attitude towards them has not changed....The coming of the Only Son of God in the midst of human history reveals God's intention to continue with the implementation of His plan despite the obstacles.[50]

Thus "the messianic mission," which consisted in "the revelation of merciful love," "is accomplished."[51]

58. If the redemptive work of Christ is not meant to make satisfaction for the sins of man but only to reveal fully the love of the Father, the classic doctrine of the Redemption must be corrected on two additional points. *Firstly,* the work of Redemption must be attributed to God the Father rather than to Christ as man:

> Christian faith in the Redemption is firstly faith in God. In Jesus Christ, His incarnate Only Son, "He whom men call God" (*i.e.,* the Father) is revealed by unveiling Himself as the only true Saviour in whom all can have faith.[52]

Jesus Christ is no longer Redeemer properly speaking. He is rather the arena where God the Father saves us, since the Love of the Father and even His name are revealed to us in Christ:

> Since God alone can forgive sins, it is God who, in Jesus his eternal Son made man, "will save his people from their sins."...The name "Jesus" signifies that the very name of God is present in the person of his Son, made man for the universal and definitive redemption from sins. It is the divine name that alone brings salvation, and henceforth all can invoke his name, for Jesus united himself to all men through his Incarnation, so that "there is no other name under heaven given among men by which we must be saved" (Acts 4:12). (CCC §§430, 432)

---

[50] International Theological Commission, *Questiones selectae de Deo Redemptore*, Dec. 8, 1994, Part IV, Nos. 40 and 42. DC 2143, Aug. 18, 1996. *Cf.* CCC §§604-605.

[51] John Paul II, *op. cit.*, No. 8.

[52] International Theological Commission, *op. cit.*, Part IV, No. 14.

59. *Secondly,* the principal act of Redemption is no longer the death of Christ but His Resurrection and his Ascension:

> Whoever speaks of the Redemption thinks firstly of the Passion and then of the Resurrection as a complement. Whoever speaks of Easter thinks firstly of the Resurrected Christ. The Resurrection no longer appears as an epilogue but rather as the end and completion of the mystery which brings us salvation.[53]

Why does the Resurrection acquire this primacy? The reason is that the Resurrection is the fullness of the revelation for which Christ became incarnate:

> The fact that Christ "was raised the third day" constitutes the final sign of the messianic mission, a sign that perfects the entire revelation of merciful love in a world that is subject to evil....In fact, Christ,...has revealed in His resurrection the fullness of the love that the Father has for Him and, in Him, for all people. "He is not God of the dead, but of the living."[54]

In this teaching, so we are told, "we have rediscovered what we can call the paschal dynamism."[55] This mystery remains the mystery of the Cross, but of the Cross "seen in the fullness of its wonderful fruitfulness, *i.e.,* insofar as it includes the Resurrection of Christ, His Ascension into glory, and the showering of all the marvellous gifts upon man through Christ who has himself become *pneuma,* life-giving Spirit."[56] Considered as a revelation "radiating outwards," the Paschal mystery is thereby identified with "Christ-*pneuma,*" called again *Kyrios.* The "*Kyrios*" is the Lord since the moment of His "Passover," who "has passed from the mortal life of this world to the glorious life of the heavens...who has broken the boundaries of time...and whose saving work, which henceforth transcends earthly time, can rediscover a 'presence' or 'actuality' in the sacramental and liturgical mysteries."[57]

---

[53] Aimon-Marie Roguet, *op. cit.,* p.11.

[54] John Paul II, *op. cit.,* No. 8.

[55] Jean Gaillard, "*Le mystère pascal dans le renouveau liturgique,*" LMD 67, 3rd Trimester 1961, p.36. (Gaillard was a member of the *Consilium.*)

[56] Louis Bouyer, *La vie de la liturgie, Lex orandi* collection (Paris: Cerf, 1956), 117. *Cf.* Bouyer, "Mysterion" in *Supplément de la Vie spirituelle* 23, November 15, 1952, p.402.

[57] Jean Gaillard, "*La liturgie du mystère pascal,*" LMD 67, 3rd Trimester 1961, p.72.

The full revelation of the Covenant is found in fact in the glorified Christ together with His body, the Church, which is without stain or wrinkle: "The mystery is Christ, but Christ including in himself his entire Body, the Church, making as it were Christ's plenitude. The mystery is, therefore, the recapitulation of humanity in itself and with God in the Body of His Son."[58] Whence the statement of John Paul II: "The Paschal Mystery is Christ at the summit of the revelation of the inscrutable mystery of God."[59]

II. THE SECOND VATICAN COUNCIL

60. The doctrine of the Paschal mystery was very much present at Vatican II, if not in the form of statements by the Magisterium, at least as a general atmosphere influencing the various constitutions. Throughout all these documents, only twice is it stated that sin offends God: in *Sacrosanctum Concilium* §109 and *Lumen Gentium* §11, while sin is described 27 times as being harmful to man and to civil and ecclesiastical society. Nowhere is it said that sin creates a debt in justice towards God, or that it is an obstacle to God's love for us. On the contrary, the Father has never ceased to look upon man with love, despite his becoming a sinner (*Lumen Gentium* §2, *Gaudium et Spes* §§2, 19). Moreover, the sufferings that result from sin (the "many evils") as well as the tendency to sin cannot come from God: "For when man looks into his own heart he finds that he is drawn towards what is wrong and sunk in many evils which cannot come from his good Creator" (*Gaudium et Spes* §13). In the texts concerning the work of Christ, not once do we see the idea of satisfaction. Though it is affirmed that the Church is His Body, and that the members of His Body share in the mysteries of the Head (*Lumen Gentium* §7), not once is it added that the Head suffers the punishments deserved by the members of His Body.

61. *Lumen Gentium*'s synthesis of the mystery of Redemption echoes the new theology:

---

[58] Louis Bouyer, "Mysterion" in *Supplément de la Vie spirituelle* 23, November 15, 1952, p.402.

[59] John Paul II, *op. cit.*, No. 8.

The eternal Father, in accordance with the utterly gratuitous and mysterious design of his wisdom and goodness, created the whole universe, and chose to raise up men to share in his own divine life; and when they had fallen in Adam, he did not abandon them, but at all times held out to them the means of salvation bestowed in consideration of Christ, the Redeemer, "who is the image of the invisible God, the firstborn of every creature" and predestined before time began "to become conformed to the image of his Son, that he should be the firstborn among many brethren" (Rom. 8:29). He determined to call together in a holy Church those who should believe in Christ (§2).

In this text, the unchanged love of the Father is described as the principal agent of our salvation (*cf. Gaudium et Spes* §41) while Christ is presented as the Redeemer insofar as He is the image which visibly reveals the mystery of God. No reference is made to satisfaction. The allusion to predestination from all eternity reinforces the idea that sin hardly interferes with the work of Christ. Thus, henceforth, the Cross will be "the sign of God's universal love" (*Nostrae Aetate* §4).

62. If the heart of the doctrine concerning the Paschal mystery (the putting aside of the vicarious satisfaction of Christ) was not explicitly declared by the Council, this was later done in a document of the International Theological Commission which resorted to caricature ("merciless God") to minimize its denial:

> The death of Jesus is not the act of a merciless God glorifying supreme sacrifice; it is not the "price of redemption" paid to some repressive alien power. It is the time and place where a God who is love and who loves us, is made visible. Jesus crucified declares how God loves us and proclaims through this gesture of love that one man has unconditionally consented to the ways of God.[60]

When it addresses the theses of Rahner, this document has reservations about a number of points; on the other hand, it explicitly accepts his refusal of vicarious satisfaction as a valid doctrine:

> [Rahner] depicts Christ as the unsurpassable symbol which shows God's will to save us. As a symbolic reality, Christ repre-

---

[60]   International Theological Commission, *op. cit.*, Part II, No.14.

sents at one and the same time the irrevocable self-giving of God according to grace, and the welcoming of that self-giving by humanity. Rahner is more reticent about the idea of expiatory sacrifice which he calls an old, *a priori* concept. Such an idea was valuable in the time of the New Testament but "not helpful today to understand what we are seeking," namely the causal effect of the meaning of the death of Jesus. According to Rahner's theory of quasi-sacramental causality, God's will to save us postulates a sign, which is in this case the death of Jesus and his Resurrection, and in and by this sign, it causes what is signified....The theory of Rahner has the undeniable merit of highlighting the loving initiative of God and the confidence and gratitude which constitute an appropriate response to it.[61]

III. THE APPLICATION OF THIS DOCTRINE TO THE LITURGICAL REFORM

63. The theology of the Paschal mystery has been the soul of the liturgical "restoration." The Council called for this "restoration" in which, "both texts and rites should be drawn up so as to express more clearly the holy things which they signify" (*Sacrosanctum Concilium* §21). Since what is signified—the act of Redemption—is, henceforth, considered from the perspective of the theology of the Paschal mystery, the reform of the rites "aims to...make the Paschal mystery of Christ live."[62] In this new doctrinal perspective, almost all the rites have been subject to change:

- Since God no longer regards sin as an injustice towards Himself and since He never breaks His side of the agreement with man, He is no longer asked to remit punishments due to sin, nor to appease His anger against the sinner. Thus, as we showed in Part One, all references to these punishments, or those that show fear of God, have been removed by the liturgical reform.
- Since the Redemption is seen as a full revelation of the Father's free and superabundant love for us, the response which the celebration of the liturgy embodies can only be

---

[61] International Theological Commission, *op. cit.,* Part III, No.14.
[62] Congregation for Divine Worship, Instruction *Liturgicae instaurationes,* DC 1574, Nov. 15, 1970.

one of thanksgiving and petition. The vicarious satisfaction of Christ and His mediation in prayer no longer prove
to be absolutely necessary. Such notions have, therefore,
been largely removed from the new missal, and notably
from the Eucharistic Prayers, as we have shown.

64. To profess belief in these truths regarding Redemption,
the Church had specially instituted the Feast of the Most Precious
Blood (Pope Pius IX instituted the feast which was later raised to
the rank of first class in 1933). In his apostolic letter *Inde a Primis*
issued in 1960, Pope John XXIII encouraged this devotion and
recommended the recitation of the Litany of the Precious Blood
throughout the month of July. In 1969, this feast disappeared
from the reformed liturgical calendar.[63] Following numerous
complaints,[64] a votive Mass was reintroduced, but not without
significant changes. Whereas in the traditional missal the Collect
states: "Almighty and everlasting God, who didst appoint Thine
only-begotten Son to be the Redeemer of the world, and didst
vouchsafe to be appeased by His Blood; grant, we beseech Thee,
that (by our solemn service), we may so venerate the Price of our
redemption, and by its power, be so defended from the evils of
this present life on earth, that we may enjoy its fruit for evermore
in heaven," the new missal says: "Father, by the blood of your own
Son you have set all men free and saved us from death. Continue
your work of love within us, that by constantly celebrating the
mystery of our salvation we may reach the eternal life it promises."

The Father, rather than the Son, brings about universal Redemption by pure love, the fruits of which are obtained by com-
memorating the mystery. This new concept of the Paschal mystery has overtaken the classic concept of the Redemption.

65. We can, therefore, see that the differences between the
two missals are nothing other than a reflection in the liturgy of
two divergent doctrines. One doctrine—the view of classic theol-

---

[63] Motu proprio *Mysteri Paschalis*, Feb. 14, 1969.
[64] Annibale Bugnini, *La riforma liturgica* (Rome: Edizioni liturgiche, 1983),
p.312.

ogy—describes the expiatory value of the death of Christ as essential to the work of Redemption. The other—the view of the new theology—considers the expiatory value of Christ's death to be a theological opinion incompatible with the goodness of God. In Part Three we will pass judgment on this disagreement.

CHAPTER 2

THE SACRAMENT
AS MYSTERY

"[Through the sacraments] the Spirit makes present and communicates the Father's work, fulfilled by the beloved Son" (CCC §1155).

66. The doctrine of the Paschal mystery not only claims to correct the negative aspects of the classic theology of the Redemption, it also means to bring about a synthesis of certain truths previously perceived as being too fragmented. The new notion of "mystery" takes pains to suppress the distinction which classic theology makes between "objective Redemption"—salvation wrought historically by Christ—and "subjective Redemption" by which we participate in the process of salvation.

> When one speaks of Redemption, one enters the context of dogmatic theology which is interested in objectively interpreting the economy of salvation, without being overly concerned about how we can participate in it....The Paschal mystery, on the other hand, takes root in the Hebrew Passover, which designated at one and the same time the unique event of salvation and its ritual commemoration renewed each year. The word mystery...refers both to God's plan, which is revealed to us, and to the concrete means by which the work of salvation is released in us. [65]

In this chapter, we will focus our attention on this new notion of "mystery" insofar as it is meant to explain the Christian's participation in Christ's work of salvation.

I. THE NOTION OF MYSTERY

(A) The New Theology

67. The new theological vision of the Paschal mystery, which culminates in the liturgical reform, finds its origin in the works of

---

[65] Aimon-Marie Roguet, *op. cit.,* p.12.

Odo Casel, a monk of Maria Laach. Despite certain controversies caused by his writings, the new theology considers the "doctrine of mysteries" to be in its substance "perhaps the most fertile theological idea of our century."[66] Fundamentally this doctrine consists in restoring to the word "sacrament" (*sacramentum* in Latin) all the semantic value possessed by the original Greek term "*mysterion*."[67] This word, which originally meant a secret reality, quickly acquires a religious connotation in ancient religions. It refers to a revelation of a transcendent being, which is real, albeit partial and veiled. To be a mystery and no longer a completely unknown object, the *res sacra occulta* (the hidden, sacred reality) must in some way come down to our level of understanding; it ought to reveal itself while still hiding beneath a veil to remain secret. In Christian vocabulary, the word "*mysterion*" will often be translated by a word with a different etymology, "*sacramentum*." Medieval scholasticism continued to give the word "mystery" its classical sense, but it used the word "sacrament" to mean only "an efficacious sign of grace," hence, the "seven sacraments." It thus conformed itself to the maxim which, in the time of St. Thomas, already summed up sacramental theology: *Sacramenta id efficiunt quod figurant*, "the sacraments produce what they signify."

68. This scholastic distinction is, however, the one which Odo Casal refuses to accept since he considers it simplistic. According to him, the Fathers of the 2nd and 3rd centuries did not think of "sacrament" as an instrument which produces grace, but rather as a symbolic image which makes the sanctifying reality really present, *re-praesentat*. A sacrament thus understood becomes a symbol which makes the *res sacra occulta* visible, not only because it signifies it in the order of knowledge, but above all because it contains it and makes it objectively present. A sacrament is no longer a sign which *produces* grace, but a symbol which *con-*

---

[66] Joseph Ratzinger, *Die sakramentale Bergrundung christlicher Existenz* (Freising: Edition Kyrios, March 1966). *Cf.* Irénée-Henri Dalmais, in *L'Eglise en prière*, under the direction of Aimé-Georges Martimort (Desclée, 1983), Vol. I, p.276; Aimon-Marie Roguet, LMD, 14, 2nd Trimester 1948, p.102; Jean Gaillard, LMD, 67, 3rd Trimester 1961, p.36, *etc.*

[67] *Cf.* Burkhard Neunheuser, article "*Mysterio*," NDL, p.110. (Neunheuser was a member of the *Consilium* and of the Congregation for Divine Worship.)

tains what it signifies, namely, the *res sacra occulta*. In place of the definition of a sacrament by its efficacy—a sign producing grace – another definition must be substituted: "[It is the] presence beneath the veil of symbols of the divine act which brings salvation."[68] The meaning of the verb *efficere* in the expression "*Sacramenta id efficiunt quod figurant*" is thereby modified. It no longer means "to produce an effect," but rather "to make something present in reality."[69]

> The mystery (*i.e.*, all the sacraments taken as a whole and also considered in isolation), is not the particular application of graces which derive from the historical act by which Christ saves us; it posits in a sacramental way the reality of the work of salvation; from the reality flows the effect.[70]

69. This new sense of the word "sacrament" is very generic since it includes all of "visible reality, belonging in itself to the world of experience, but re-presenting (making present) supernatural realities for man."[71] It applies to the liturgy, and at a higher level to Christ and to the Church.

● If God Himself is the *res sacra occulta* par excellence, He becomes mystery insofar as He reveals Himself to man. Christ is, therefore, the "primordial sacrament"[72] since "Christ—the very fulfillment of the messianic prophecy—...makes present and thus more fully reveals the Father."[73]

● The Church is in its turn considered as a sacrament. In the same way that Christ is the sacrament of God, since it is by Him and in Him that God enters history and, moreover, since it is Christ who concretely represents Him before men, so the Church, continuing this process, is the sacrament of Christ, because it is the reality on earth in which

---

[68] Odo Casal, JLW, VIII, p.145.

[69] Odo Casal, JLW, XV, p.233.

[70] Odo Casal, JLW, XIII, p.123.

[71] Jean-Hervé Nicolas, *Synthèse dogmatique. De la Trinité à la Trinité*, (Fribourg: Editions universitaires, 1985), p.630.

[72] *Cf.* Edouard Schillebeeckx, *Le Christ, sacrement de la rencontre avec Dieu*, collection *Lex orandi* (Paris: Cerf, 1964), p.22.

[73] John Paul II, *op. cit.*, No. 3.

and through which man can meet Christ and God in Christ.[74]

● Moreover, the liturgy in its entirety becomes a sacrament. Through the "mystery of worship," "Christ in glory" (or "*Kyrios*") a glory achieved through His Ascension, continues to make Himself present to men, so that they may come to their salvation by experiencing His presence.

> The reactualization of the mystery of salvation which happens in the mysteries of the Church's worship assures a real contact between each believer and the historical event of Easter, notwithstanding the boundaries of earthly time. Christ in glory continues to touch and to sanctify men throughout history by the very action of his historical deeds.[75]

● Finally, the people assembled for the liturgical celebration are in a certain way the sacrament of the Church. The assembly manifests the Church and makes it present. "Here on earth the liturgical assembly is the most expressive manifestation and a veritable epiphany of the Church; the assembly shows and reveals it....The voice of the assembly is the voice of the Church, the Spouse of Christ."[76]

70. These are the first fruits of developing Casel's theology. The Catechism of 1992 explains:

> The Greek word *mysterion* was translated into Latin by two terms: *mysterium* and *sacramentum*. In later usage the term *sacramentum* emphasizes the visible sign of the hidden reality of salvation which was indicated by the term *mysterium*. In this sense, Christ himself is the mystery of salvation: "For there is no other mystery of God, except Christ" (St. Augustine). The saving work of his holy and sanctifying humanity is the sacrament of salvation, which is revealed and active in the Church's sacraments (which the Eastern Churches also call "the holy mysteries"). The seven sacraments are the signs and instruments by

---

[74] Jean-Hervé Nicolas, *op. cit.,* p.635.
[75] Jean Gaillard, *Le mystère pascal dans le renouveau liturgique,* LMD, 67, 3rd Trimester, 1961, p.72.
[76] Aimé-Georges Martimort, *L'Eglise en prière* (Desclée, 1965), p.92.

which the Holy Spirit spreads the grace of Christ the head throughout the Church which is his Body. The Church, then, both contains and communicates the invisible grace she signifies. It is in this analogical sense, that the Church is called a "sacrament" (CCC §774).

The same Catechism insists on the fact that the very work of salvation is present in the holy mysteries, and implies that the sanctifying action of the sacraments flows from this presence beneath the veil of symbol.[77]

(B) The Second Vatican Council

71. Official acceptance of this new understanding of the word "sacrament" dates from Vatican II. Starting with the Constitution on the Liturgy, it plays a vital role. Without actually using the word, the idea that Christ is the sacrament of God is expressed in quasi-patristic or quasi-scriptural language (*Sacrosanctum Concilium* §5). The Church appears as *sacramentum* derived from the primordial *sacramentum* which is Christ himself: "For it was from the side of Christ as he slept the sleep of death upon the cross that there came forth 'the wondrous sacrament of the whole Church.'"

Moreover, the Council describes the nature of, and sets, the liturgy in the context of this sacramentality of the Church (Christ "always present in his Church," *Sacrosanctum Concilium* §7). In his commentary on the Constitution, Vagaggini writes: "For the first time in a document of the Magisterium, the structure of the liturgy, the system of efficacious signs of sanctification and of worship, is thrown into relief against the notion of sacrament."[78] This notion of sacrament also guides conciliar ecclesiology: (*Lumen Gentium* §1): ...the Church, in Christ, is in the nature of sacrament—a sign and instrument, that is, of Communion with God and of unity among all men...." How is the Church a sacrament? She is a sacrament by making Christ present for us: "...the Church, a pilgrim now on earth, is necessary for salvation: the one Christ is mediator and the way of salvation; he is present to us in his body which is the Church" (*Lumen Gentium* §14).

---

[77] *Cf.* CCC §§1076, 1104, 1364.

[78] Cyprien Vagaggini, "*La Constitution de Vatican II sur la liturgie,*" *Paroisse et liturgie*, 65, 1964, p.36. [Vagaggini was a member of the *Consilium* and of the International Theological Commission.]

II. THE MYSTERY AS THE ARENA OF REVELATION

(A) The New Theology

72. The new theology gives such importance to the "*mysterion*" in the theology of the liturgy because it believes this notion enables it to solve the issues raised by modern thought. Contemporary thinking, conditioned largely by Kantism, has abandoned the principles of realist philosophy and questions the value of speculative knowledge. Modern man, made dizzy by the abyss of idealism, attaches himself all the more to the value of experience which seems to enable him to make direct contact with reality. He is tempted by scepticism and avid to see and touch, and moreover appears disappointed with traditional doctrine. This doctrine asserts that the Church is indeed founded on a unique experience, *i.e.,* the visit of God to His people (Lk. 1:68). It states that Jesus Christ shared our human existence, and revealed His doctrine of salvation in both words and deeds: "For I have given you an example, that as I have done to you, you may do also" (Jn. 13:15). At the same time the Church teaches that this fundamental experience was the exclusive privilege of the first Christians who spoke with Christ. Other Christians must draw upon this source to live their own lives, but they do this only through the testimony of the Apostles: "That which we have seen and have heard, we declare unto you, that you also may have fellowship with us…" (I Jn. 1:3). Revelation is, therefore, a doctrine transmitted by preaching, *fides ex auditu* (Rom. 10:17) since only words are communicable. Actions by definition pass away. Moreover, "…blessed are those who have not seen and have believed" (Jn. 20:29). Such an idea seems difficult to accept for modern thought because it first requires belief in the mediation of the Church and in her infallibility in matters of Faith. The new theology, therefore, wants to present Revelation in a way that better meets the expectations of modern man. It maintains that God does not reveal Himself in a doctrine but rather in an experience of His presence. It then explains how this experience was not the privilege of the first believers but is given to all men, especially through the liturgy.

73. According to the new theology, Revelation is not merely a series of abstract statements which form a doctrinal system. Reve-

lation comes about especially through a living contact with the
mystery of divinity: "The notion of *mysterion* seeks to express the
character of God's direct revelation to His servants which is linked
to Revelation; this stands in contrast with a philosophical type of
knowledge."[79] In other words, God does not reveal Himself to
man only "in words"—considered as human concepts containing
knowledge of the mystery of God—but "in words and deeds,"
i.e., by means of *divine actions* which make the mysterious reality
of God present to man:

> Christianity, in the full and original sense of the word ("Gos-
> pel of God" or "Gospel of Christ"), is not, therefore, a particular
> view of the world set against a religious background, nor a reli-
> gious or theological system of doctrines, nor is it simply a moral
> law: it is a *mystery* in the Paulinian sense of the word. It is the
> revelation of God to humanity. It is God who acts to reveal
> Himself in theandric deeds and gestures filled with life and
> strength, and in deeds and actions which, by this revelation and
> the communication of grace, make it possible for humanity to
> approach the Divinity.[80]

74. Even these words can seem audacious to modern man
since today the very possibility of Revelation is open to doubt; by
rejecting the natural realism of the human mind, idealist philosophies have endangered man's access to realities which transcend
the order of pure phenomena. How does one go from mystical
experience to divine revelation? Is there not an unwarranted progression from the phenomenon to God's absolute? The doctrine
of mysteries again believes it can answer this "great challenge at
the end of this millennium," the challenge "to move from *phenomenon* to *foundation*, a step as necessary as it is urgent."[81] It presents the phenomenon as a "symbol," which, by means of a suit-
able interpretation, enables man to have objective contact with
the transcendental realities it "symbolizes." The new theology
thereby relies on the schools of modern symbolist[82] thought
which are often explicitly quoted.[83] The 1992 Catechism is very

[79] Odo Casel, *Le mystère du culte*, [*The Mystery of Christian Worship*], collection *Lex orandi*, (Paris: Cerf, 1964), p.300.
[80] Odo Casel, *op. cit.,* p.300.
[81] John Paul II, *Fides et Ratio*, Sept. 14, 1998, No. 83.

much marked by this philosophical tendency. Near the beginning of the section on "the sacramental celebration of the Paschal mystery" eight paragraphs are devoted to the notion of "signs and symbols" (CCC §§1145-52) stating that, "man perceives spiritual realities through physical signs and symbols" (CCC §1146).

The following paragraphs describe the slow evolution of religious hermeneutics which Christ brought to maturity by giving a new and definitive sense to already existing signs (CCC §1151; *cf.* §1115).

75. By adopting this thinking, the new theology is immediately at odds with classic theology. The Fathers of the Church never in fact questioned the objective value of speculative knowledge. They had no difficulties in accepting Revelation as a set of propositions received *ex auditu,* and their theological investigations sought only to solve the ontological problems raised by each mystery, *e.g.,* the consubstantiality of the Divine Persons, the hypostatic union of the natures of Christ, *etc.* Knowledge of the mysteries was always considered in second place, and as a consequence of their being. By questioning the realist perspective, the new theology profoundly changes sacramental theology, and this change takes the form of a re-interpretation of the traditional definition of a sacrament. Though the expression "efficacious sign of sanctification" is kept, it acquires another value. Instead of looking upon a sacrament in the ontological order as an instrumental, efficient cause of grace sanctifying the soul, the new theology will henceforth look upon a sacrament from the perspective of human

---

[82] For *Schleiermacher,* the sacred is manifested in the symbols of myth. *Mercia Eliade* sees the mythical symbol as a "hierophany" which makes possible a mythical participation in the sacred. *Carl Jung* also grants symbols some importance as a manifestation of the collective unconsciousness. In the interpretation of *Paul Ricoeur,* symbols are an indication of the human condition at the heart of being, whence their ontological value. *Ernst Cassirer* calls man a "symbolic animal" to which corresponds a world that has become "symbolic form," *etc.* Moreover, according to *K. Langer,* the study of symbols is the new foundation on which philosophy can be based.

[83] See, for example, Cyprien Vagaggini, *Initiation à la théologie de la liturgie* (Bruges: Apostolat liturgique, 1959), Vol. I, p.40. Also, J. P. Dong, *L'Eucharistie comme réalité symbolique,* collection *Cogitatio fidei* (Cerf, 1972).

knowledge, hence making it a "manifestation" or a "revelation" of the living presence of God; the theory is that if man enters thus into contact with God, his sanctification will thereby be wrought.

76. Looked upon in this way, the liturgy becomes the arena of Revelation which is transmitted to man by means of a rite. The symbolism of this rite enables man to have a living contact with the God who reveals. While classic theology teaches that Tradition is guaranteed by the Magisterium of the Church, the *Paradosis* or Tradition is now guaranteed by a living contact with God. This is why the notion of "living Tradition" is henceforth readily identified with the mysteries of the liturgy.

> In the Christian religion, the great deeds of God, thus the events and works, form the substance of the *Paradosis*. What we have received in the *Paradosis*, we commemorate in the liturgy, and thus make present the mysteries of the deeds which save us. This is the meaning of the liturgy for us. We say the sacred formulae contained in divine Revelation, but in these, the Church does not merely pass on information in the speculative order. She declares the treasure of the faith, giving it to us in a living manner through the sacred rites and prayers.[84]

Thus "by celebrating the liturgical acts (sacraments, sacramentals, hearing of the Word), Christians (priests and faithful) experience in a certain way the truths of the faith as proclaimed and celebrated in the liturgy. This is a special mode of knowledge by experience or participation."[85] This vision is considerably developed in the 1992 Catechism. Revelation does not consist of so many human words, but in the unique Word of God: "The Son is his Father's definitive Word; so there will be no further Revelation after him" (CCC §73). The Christian's faith must, therefore, be informed by living contact with the Word, a contact brought about most effectively not by preaching, but by the liturgical celebration of the Paschal mystery:

> [The liturgy] is therefore the privileged place for catechizing the People of God....Liturgical catechesis aims to initiate people into the mystery of Christ ("mystagogy") by proceeding from

---

[84] Odo Casel, *op. cit.*, p.302.
[85] Jean Gaillard, *op. cit.*, p.70.

the visible to the invisible, from the sign to the thing signified, from the "sacraments" to the "mysteries" (CCC §1074-75).

(B) The Second Vatican Council

77. If Vatican II did not explicitly declare the liturgy to be the arena of Revelation, it nevertheless ratified the principle behind it, namely, the new understanding of Revelation in "words and deeds": "This economy of Revelation is realized by words and deeds, which are intrinsically bound up with each other. As a result, the works performed by God in the history of salvation show forth and bear out the doctrine and realities signified by the words; the words, for their part, proclaim the works, and bring to light the mystery they contain" (*Dei Verbum* §2). Revelation is not only, therefore, the Gospel preached by Christ, but Christ Himself as the manifestation of God: "[The Christ] himself—to see whom is to see the Father (*cf.* Jn. 14:9)—completed and perfected Revelation and confirmed it with divine guarantees. He did this by the total fact of his presence and self-manifestation—by words and works, signs and miracles, but above all by his death and glorious resurrection from the dead, and finally by sending the Spirit of truth" (*Dei Verbum* §4). This idea will later be developed by the International Theological Commission:

> The Revelation attested to in Sacred Scripture was accomplished through words and deeds in the history of God's relations with man. The truth revealed, as taught by Sacred Scripture, is the truth of a God who shows that He is faithful throughout all history; ultimately it is the Father's communicating Himself in Jesus Christ in view of the permanent action of the Holy Spirit....This is why Jesus Christ is, for a Christian, the unique Word present in the multiplicity of words.[86]

---

[86] International Theological Commission, *L'interprétation des dogmes*, 1988, DC 2006, May 20, 1990, p.492.

III. APPLICATION OF THIS DOCTRINE
TO THE LITURGICAL REFORM

(A) The Sacraments of the Faith

78. According to this new understanding, the sacraments, the arenas of Divine Revelation, will demand faith from the assembly in a different way. Since the sacrament is considered from the perspective of human knowledge, it must be interpreted—through the faith—to make the signified reality present to the participants. Only an act of faith in the course of the rite seems to enable one to penetrate the symbolism of the sacrament and reach the mystery, thus ensuring the action of the mystery on the soul.[87] When, on the other hand, classic theology says that the sacraments produce grace *ex opere operato* in the soul, it teaches that although supernatural faith is necessary for someone to receive the sacraments fruitfully, this faith only need bring the soul to submit itself to the action of the Church; a full understanding of the meaning of the sacramental sign is by no means absolutely necessary.

79. The participants come into contact with the mystery through faith, and the mystery is Revelation. The mystery, therefore, seems mainly to concern the virtue of faith. As Casel says:

> What we have received in the *Paradosis*, we commemorate in the liturgy and thus make present the mysteries of the deeds which save us. This is the meaning of the liturgy for us. We say the sacred formulae contained in divine Revelation [in which] the Church...declares to us the treasure of the faith, giving it to us in a living manner through the sacred rites and prayers....The celebration of the mysteries emerges, therefore, as a masterfully designed religious service which leads to the ecstatic contemplation of the divinity.[88]

---

[87] Admittedly the faith of the Church is said to be active and anterior to the individual's faith (CCC §1124); but later on the Church is said to be made present and effective by the assembly of the faithful (CCC §§1140-41). It is, therefore, an act of faith on the part of the community during the rite which enables them to experience the mystery which has been made present and which ensures the mystery's power to sanctify them.

[88] Odo Casel, *op. cit.*, p.302.

The commentary Casel makes on the Postcommunion prayer on the octave day of the Epiphany is indicative of his vision:

> "Prevent us always and in all places with Thy heavenly light, we beseech the, O Lord: that we may discern with a pure vision, and receive with worthy affections, the mystery in which Thou wouldst have us partake." What does this partaking consist of? *Firstly of contemplation.* We contemplate the mystery in the gnosis of the faith. This is not, however, an inactive and ineffective contemplation. We are transformed by this contemplation.[89]

80. This understanding of sacrament seems to be the origin of the profound, liturgical changes relating to the sacrificial offering as analyzed in Part One. If we look upon a sacrament primarily as the actuation of faith, it is logical to speak no longer of the act of the Sovereign Priest who offers Himself to His Father in the person of His minister (this act of Christ only requires of us habitual faith), and to lay emphasis on the act whereby the assembly offers the Body and Blood of Christ present on the altar. Only this second offering involves an attitude of faith:

> The manner in which man, by Christ and through Christ – "by the offering of the Body of the Lord"—offers himself and the world to the Father, expresses simply and fundamentally the existential essence of the Faith. In faith, as Vatican II teaches, man "abandons himself totally to God" in responding to the revelation God has made of Himself. This abandonment, which is part of the very essence of faith, is brought almost to its fullness in the attitude which comes from participating in Christ's priesthood. In fact, such an attitude seems to give to the Christian's acts of faith their most complete existential dimension. [90]

81. The Council's Constitution on the Liturgy greatly insists on the role of faith: "[The sacraments] not only presuppose faith, but by words and objects they also nourish, strengthen, and express it. That is why they are called sacraments of faith" (*Sacrosanctum* §59). One theologian, commenting on this text, writes:

---

[89] Odo Casel, *op. cit.,* p.319.
[90] Karol Wojtyla, *Aux sources du renouveau, étude sur la mise en oeuvre de Vatican II* (Centurion, 1979), p.184. [Wojtyla was a member of the Congregation for Divine Worship.]

If the Council of Trent defined the power of the sacraments in terms of the "work worked" (*ex opere operato*), it did not intend thereby to deny the necessity of having faith in order to be justified or to receive the sacraments, nor did it intend to deny the psychological power of the sacraments, the only sacramental power the Protestants accept insofar as it stirs and excites faith. This particular power [of the sacraments] is the one Vatican II wanted to emphasize.[91]

The 1992 Catechism seems to reflect this vision when explaining the expression *ex opere operato:*

> Celebrated worthily in faith, the sacraments confer the grace that they signify. They are efficacious because in them Christ himself is at work: it is he who baptizes, he who acts in his sacraments in order to communicate the grace that each sacrament signifies. The Father always hears the prayer of his Son's Church, which, in the *epiclesis* of each sacrament, expresses her faith in the power of the Spirit. As fire transforms into itself everything it touches, so the Holy Spirit transforms into the divine life whatever is subjected to his power (CCC §1127).

In the theological context of the 1992 Catechism, it is easy to understand that the sacrament draws its power from the re-presentation of the deeds which bring about our salvation ("it is he who acts"), which give their saving power to the Church through a contact ("as fire transforms into itself everything it touches") of faith ("celebrated worthily in faith," "[the Church] expresses her faith in the power of the Spirit"), which is efficacious ("transforms into the divine life whatever is subjected to his power"). This interpretation is reinforced by the context of these lines; the sacraments are "sacraments of salvation" (CCC §§1127-29) only after being "sacraments of faith" (CCC §§1122-26) because "the liturgical assembly is first of all a Communion in faith" (CCC §1102).

(B) A New Place for the Word of God

82. If the new theology has neglected the power of the sacraments and emphasized instead their meaning as nourishment for faith, the opposite has happened as regards Sacred Scripture; the

---

[91] M. Nicolau, *Teologia del signo sacramental,* BAC, 1969, p.367

emphasis here is now laid on its power rather than on its meaning. In fact the conciliar Constitution on the Liturgy even went as far as to apply to Scripture the new notion of sacramental mystery: "He is present in his word since it is he himself who speaks when the holy scriptures are read in the Church" (*Sacrosanctum Concilium* §7). Henceforth the Word of God is classed among those tangible signs through which "it involves the presentation of man's sanctification under the guise of signs perceptible by the senses and its accomplishment in ways appropriate to each of these signs" (*ibid.*).[92] One can, therefore, apply to it the doctrine of symbolism. Contrary to the position of classic theology, Biblical readings are not meant in the first place to provide the concepts of faith with their intellectual content. To stop at the concepts of faith would be to remain at the level of the sign, without passing beyond to what they signify. The faith must look beneath the symbolic veil of words to find Christ Himself made present. Is He not the "definitive Word of God" (CCC §73)? Scripture seen in this way is no longer meant for the instruction of faith, a faith from which mystical experience can flow. Now Scripture is meant to produce mystical experience, an experience which is supposed to nourish knowledge of the faith.

83. This singular way of looking at Sacred Scripture explains the parallel the new missal draws between the Liturgy of the Word and the Eucharistic Liturgy:

> Today liturgical historians largely agree that the Liturgy of the Word and the Eucharistic Liturgy go back to a rite of Jewish origin....The Christian community adopted the essential structure of this celebration. The proclamation of the Word comes first, but it must be recognized that the theology underpinning this was until now only a personal opinion lacking official recognition. Vatican II corroborates this perspective, without making it a doctrine of the Faith; "Christ is present in his Word." During the Reformation, the Church considered herself obliged to speak especially about Christ's presence in the Eucharist; she forgot, therefore, that there were other modes of the Lord's presence parallel to the sacramental presence....This is why the

---

[92] Here the French translation seems to differ significantly from the English version by Flannery. See the Latin.— *Translator's note.*

Council insists on the immense importance of Sacred Scripture in the celebration of the liturgy. [93]

Thus it is that "the Eucharistic table set for us is the table both of the Word of God and of the Body of the Lord" (CCC §1346). The 1992 Catechism goes so far as to grant a certain primacy to the "Word" because it determines the meaning of other symbols:

> A sacramental celebration is a meeting of God's children with their Father, in Christ and the Holy Spirit; this meeting takes the form of a dialogue, through actions and words. Admittedly, the symbolic actions are already a language, but the Word of God and the response of faith have to accompany and give life to them, so that the seed of the Kingdom can bear its fruit in good soil. The liturgical actions signify what the Word of God expresses: both his free initiative and his people's response of faith (CCC §1153).

(C) Conclusion

84. This concept of *mysterion* according to which a sacrament makes divine realities present and gives them to man to nourish his faith, has been, therefore, one of the main lines of the liturgical reform:

- It explains the constant parallel between the "Liturgy of the Word" and the "Eucharistic Liturgy" both of which are the "table of the Lord" (IG §§43, 56) where Christ gives Himself as spiritual food (IG §§33, 56).
- It explains the lessening of the worship of the Real Presence during Mass. The Eucharistic presence is no longer firstly recognized in itself, but principally insofar as it nourishes faith.
- It explains the greater emphasis laid on the common priesthood of the faithful. The sacrificial oblation is considered almost exclusively from the point of view of the oblation taken in its restricted sense which constitutes the only response of faith.

---

[93] Adrien Nocent, "*Sobre la reforma del ordinario de la Misa*" in *La sagrada liturgia renovada por el Concilio*, under the direction of G. Barauna, (Madrid: Studium, 1965), p.489.

● It explains the new way of looking at the Eucharist as the *mysterium fidei.*

Both in its descent (described as revelation) and in its ascent (oblation), a sacrament is henceforth looked upon almost exclusively as a "sacrament of faith" designed to nourish the faith of the People of God.

CHAPTER 3

THE MEMORIAL

The Eucharist is the memorial of Christ's Passover, that is, of the work of salvation accomplished by the life, death, and resurrection of Christ, a work made present by the liturgical action (CCC §1409).

85. The doctrine of the Paschal mystery glorifies the actions of Christ as revelation more than as propitiation (Part Two, Chapter 1). It, therefore, considers the sacraments as means of making the actions of Christ present—those which reveal the love of the Father—rather than efficacious means of salvation which apply to us the merits of Christ (Part Two, Chapter 2). This change of perspective renders somewhat obsolete the clearly sacrificial character which the Mass previously bore. The liturgical reform has also brought the memorial aspect of the Mass into the foreground since it maintains that the memorial makes present the reality it commemorates. The liturgical celebration is, therefore, a proclamation of thanksgiving, and a declaration and revelation of the mysteries which are commemorated. In other words, the liturgical celebration is a continuation and diffusion of Christ's mission of salvation, since this mission is, henceforth, looked upon as a revelation "in words and deeds." The notion of memorial thus becomes the key to interpreting the entire liturgy:

> The entire liturgy is nothing but a memorial of the Savior's actions in an objective sense. At the same time it is a development and fulfillment of the *anamnesis* of the Mass....Removing this keystone from the structure of the liturgy would cause it to collapse leaving nothing but meaningless rubble. One can thus easily see the importance of clearly understanding the *anamnesis* of the Canon of the Mass; it is like a seed which potentially contains all the wealth and development of the liturgy.[94]

---

[94] Odo Casel, *Faites ceci en mémoire de moi,* collection *Lex orandi* (Paris: Paris, 1962), pp.10,11.

We will now, therefore, analyze what the new theology understands by "memorial," and seek to clarify in particular the link it wishes to keep with the sacrificial dimension of the Mass.

I. THE MASS AS A MEMORIAL

86. The new theology is wary of intellectual systematization and prefers to consider revealed mysteries from a historical point of view, *i.e.,* as living realities which operate and develop through the history of salvation. Thus it analyzes the New Testament in the light of the Old: "The authors and messengers of the New Testament—Jesus and the Apostles—who belong to the cultural context of the Old Testament and share fully its spirituality, can only be understood by referring initially to the Old Testament."[95] Returning to the Jewish Passover is, therefore, necessary in order to understand the essential nature of the Eucharist. Now, we are told[96] that the ritual of the ancient Passover was essentially a memorial of three things; Israel *remembered* the miraculous liberation from Egypt and prayed to God in hymns of thanksgiving—in a "eucharist"—for the help He gave to His people. This, however, was not the simple memorial of a bygone action; in fact this memory—or *anamnesis*—was not purely subjective because it also meant that God remembered His people and made Himself present among them to renew His work of salvation:

On the night of the Passover, not only does Israel remember Yahweh and His salvation, but Yahweh remembers Israel and His faithful servants. Yahweh's remembering means, according to late, Jewish Biblical conceptions, a way for God to be present again and to bring His salvation anew.[97]

The memorial was, therefore, *objective, i.e.,* it was the actualization and declaration of the Covenant before God and man. The Jews, however, knew that the Covenant they celebrated was

---

[95] Pietro Sorci, article, *"Mistero pasquale,"* NDL, p.832.

[96] *Cf.* Marsili, *"La misa, misterio pascual y misterio de la Iglesia,"* in *La sagrada liturgia renovada por el Concilio*, under the direction of G. Barauna (Madrid: Studium, 1965), pp.468-470. (Marsili was director of Saint Anselm's Pontifical Institute for the Liturgy.) Pietro Sorci, article *"Mistero pasquale,"* NDL, p.839.

[97] N. Fluglister quoted by Burkhard Neunheuser, article *"Memoriale,"* NDL, p.772. *Cf.* Louis Bouyer, *Eucharistie* (Desclée, 1990), p.88.

not yet fully realized: Israel was awaiting the Messiah. The rite of the Passover also had a third dimension which was both *prophetic* and eschatological. The Jewish Passover thus consisted of the memorial of a deed which had saved them, the declaration and eucharistic celebration of the present Covenant, and a prophecy of the future fulfillment of God's promises.

87. Since Christ adopted the rite of the old Passover when He instituted the Eucharist during the paschal meal, and given, moreover, that only the memorial aspect of this rite is described, the Mass is considered firstly as the "memorial of the Lord."[98] To justify this assertion, a new interpretation of Lk. 22:19 has been put forward. In the expression, "Do this in memory of me," it is thought that:

> The stress then is laid not on the prescription: "Do this" but on the specification: "Do it (*from now on* is understood) *in memory of me*." More exactly, as Jeremias has shown these words should be translated: "Do this as my memorial"; and this word must be given the sense that it always has in the rabbinical literature and especially the liturgical literature of the period.[99]

This is why the words of consecration have been modified as we pointed out in Part One.

88. Now as we have seen, the Jewish memorial was able to make God present again and renew the effects of His salvation; it was an *objective* memorial and not simply a calling to mind of the past. This also applies then to the Eucharist. It is not a simple remembrance; it makes present the deeds by which Christ wrought salvation, and which it commemorates:

---

[98] When the 1992 Catechism refers to the sacrament of the Eucharist (CCC §§1328-32) an explanation follows every term used ("Eucharist," "The Lord's Supper," *etc.*) and each begins with the conjunction "because." When, however, it refers to the "memorial" (CCC §1330), no explanation is given, "The *memorial* of the Lord's Passion and Resurrection." Thus, according to the 1992 Catechism, "memorial" is the name which best suits this sacrament.

[99] Louis Bouyer, *op. cit.*, p.107. *Cf.* Odo Casel, *Faites ceci en mémoire de moi*, p.8.

[The eucharistic memorial] is an objective memorial and not just (though naturally it is this also) a subjective memory of what the Lord has done for us. In other words, it is a real memorial and not merely a memorial in thought, a simple, conceptual memory, a *nuda commemoratio* as the Council of Trent says when condemning Luther.[100]

The enormous importance which the doctrine of the Paschal mystery gives to the memorial dimension of the liturgy is thus apparent; within the liturgy, only the memorial is capable of expressing the new notion of a sacrament by which the events of salvation are mysteriously made present.

89. The memorial prayer of the Church must, therefore, be "a *real* prayer which signifies and makes something real. It must not, therefore, express a memory recalled solely at the subjective level. It must rather convey an *objective memory by means of an action*."[101] In order that this action should not be interpreted as the outward expression of a subjective memory, it should by nature be an action of the community, *i.e.,* a social action. This, henceforth, is how the public character of the liturgy is understood; it is a public act in the sense that it "organizes all the activities of a community of faithful and of each of its members, and puts them directly at the service of God."[102] In the case of the Mass, what communal action will be the setting for the objective memorial? The principle of the memorial coming from the old Passover and continuing in the new Passover means that this communal action will be a meal. Jesus Christ in fact instituted the Eucharistic memorial during a Jewish ritual meal.

> The celebration of the memory of the Lord and of his redeeming Passion in the course of a sacred *meal* provided the original, fundamental grounds [for the eucharistic celebration]. The meal aspect is foremost at the beginning. It was not just any meal. It was a sacred meal, sanctified not only by the memory it recalled and made sacramentally present, but also by the prayer

---

[100] Burkhard Neunheuser, article "*Memoriale,*" NDL, p.77.

[101] Odo Casel, *op. cit.,* p.9. The italics are in the text.

[102] Irénée-Henri Dalmais, "La liturgie, acte de l'Eglise," LMD 19, 3rd Trimester, 1949, p.8. [Dalmais was a member of the *Consilium.*]

which was added to the memorial and which raised it up to God.[103]

90. This way of looking at the memorial of the Mass made its way into the official texts of the Church at Vatican II. From the first lines of the Constitution on the Liturgy, we find the sacrificial aspect and the memorial aspect of the Mass juxtaposed without a clear link:

> At the Last Supper, on the night he was betrayed, our Savior instituted the eucharistic sacrifice of his Body and Blood. This he did in order to perpetuate the sacrifice of the Cross throughout the ages until he should come again, and so to entrust to his beloved Spouse, the Church, a memorial of his death and resurrection: a sacrament of love, a sign of unity, a bond of charity, a paschal banquet in which Christ is consumed, the mind is filled with grace, and a pledge of future glory is given to us (*Sacrosanctum Concilium* §47).

Afterwards the Council was happy to refer to the Mass simply as "the memorial of the Lord's death and resurrection" (*Ad Gentes Divinitus* §14) for henceforth this is seemingly the most important aspect of the Eucharistic celebration:

> By a tradition handed down from the apostles, which took its origin from the very day of Christ's resurrection, the Church celebrates the Paschal mystery every seventh day, which day is appropriately called the Lord's Day or Sunday. For on this day Christ's faithful are bound to come together into one place. They should listen to the word of God and take part in the Eucharist, thus calling to mind the passion, resurrection, and glory of the Lord Jesus, and giving thanks to God... (*Sacrosanctum Concilium* §106).

---

[103] Joseph-André Jungmann, *Missarum solemnia* (Aubier, 1951), Vol. I, p.44. [Jungmann was a member of the *Consilium*.] *Cf.* Romano Guardini, *Besinnung vor der Feier des hl. Messe* (Moguncia, 1939), p.76. [Guardini was a member of the Preparatory Commission on the Liturgy for the Council.]; Henri-Marie Féret, *La messe, rassemblement de la communauté*, collection *Lex orandi* (Paris: Cerf, 1947), pp.226*ff.*

II. THE MASS AS THE PASSOVER OF THE LORD

91. As the conciliar texts point out, the object of the Eucharistic memorial is the death and, at the same time, the Resurrection of the Lord. The new theology makes clear that if the memorial rite assures continuity between the two Passovers, the new Passover is superior to the Passover of the Exodus by reason of its object:

> [For Israel] every time Passover is celebrated, the Exodus events are made present to the memory of believers so that they may conform their lives to them. In the New Testament, the memorial takes on new meaning. When the Church celebrates the Eucharist, she commemorates Christ's Passover, and it is made present... (CCC §§1363-64).

The Eucharistic memorial is that of the whole work of salvation from the point of view of its dynamic and indivisible unity, which was previously underlined: "The Eucharist is the memorial of Christ's Passover, that is, of the work of salvation accomplished by the life, death, and resurrection of Christ, a work made present by the liturgical action" (CCC §1409, *cf.* §§1323, 1330, 1337, 1364). Not only are past mysteries made present, but the prophetic dimension of the Eucharist enables future mysteries to be made present also. The Eucharist then becomes a real anticipation—and not simply a promise—of the celestial liturgy:

> Beneath a sacramental veil and in the mystery of faith, the eschatological realities to be manifested at the end of time are really present. Since the liturgical assembly expresses the fullness of the mystery of the Church, it is also the real anticipation of the definitive assembly of redeemed humanity, gathered together for the Messianic banquet which seals the definitive Covenant.[104]

By the sacraments, the liturgy makes us "live from the life of the risen Christ" (CCC §1091).

92. Much more than the mysteries of Christ, it is Christ made glorious by His mysteries (the *Kyrios*) who is made present, and who acts through the sacraments:

---

[104] Irénée-Henri Dalmais, *Initiation à la liturgie*, Cahiers de la Pierre-qui-vire (Desclée, 1958). *Cf.* CCC §1326.

He [the *Kyrios*] is in effect the sole dispenser of divine life
which he henceforth gives to men, especially by means of the
sacraments; through the sacraments, and above all by the Eucharist, we receive from Christ's holy and glorified humanity—the
living instrument of his Divinity—the influx of divine life of
which this humanity is full.[105]

The emphasis is put on the *Kyrios* rather than on Christ,
Priest and Victim, and also on His Resurrection rather than on
Calvary. Since Christ is considered firstly as the sacrament of God
revealing to man the unchanged love of the Father who wishes to
share His glory, the central point in the life of Christ becomes the
Resurrection and Ascension. Here it is that

the three divine persons act together as one, and *manifest*
their own proper characteristics. The Father's power "raised up"
Christ his Son and by doing so perfectly introduced his Son's
humanity, including his body, into the Trinity. Jesus *is conclu-
sively revealed* as "Son of God in power according to the Spirit of
holiness *by his Resurrection from the dead*." St. Paul insists on the
manifestation of God's power through the working of the Spirit
who gave life to Jesus' dead humanity and called it to the glorious state of Lordship (CCC §648).

The memorial of the Mass, therefore, must admittedly recall
the death of Christ, but it must above all focus on his Resurrection.

93. These ideas are profoundly opposed to classic theology
which sees the sacrificial death of the Crucified Christ as the heart
of the work of redemption. In this death the Word Incarnate
achieves His mission with regard to God and man. He became
incarnate principally for love of the Father, and to render to God
the glory which man had refused to give. Now of all Christ's human actions the one which showed the greatest love for the
Father—by glorifying Him the most—was his obedient death on
the Cross.

● The intensity of Christ's charity was the same in all His
actions, but since "greater love than this no man hath, that
a man lay down his life for his friends" (Jn. 15:13), Christ

---

[105] Cyprien Vagaggini, "*La Consitution de Vatican II sur la liturgie*," *Paroisse et
liturgie* 65, 1964, p.39.

wanted to die to show His love for the Father, "that the world may know that I love the Father…" (Jn. 14:31).

- To glorify perfectly the Father, Christ wanted to offer Him the most perfect act of religion. Now, the perfect act of the virtue of religion is sacrifice. Christ, therefore, directed His entire human existence towards "his hour," when He would "glorify [the Father] on the earth" and accomplish the work His Father had given Him to do (Jn. 17:4).

If we consider Christ's work insofar as it benefits men, the death on the Cross is still the most important of His actions. The Resurrection certainly contributes to our salvation, notably as an example for us, but classic theology maintains that only the death of Christ—and not His Resurrection—has a meritorious and satisfactory value. Thus for classic theology, it is the Passion rather than the Resurrection which sums up our salvation.

94. Could not the solution to these doctrinal differences be found in Christ Himself? If we consider Christ's life only from the point of view of a Paschal dynamism—which reaches its fulfillment when Christ is established as "Lord" at the Ascension—does this not diminish Christ and obscure the truth that He was "Lord" from the moment of His Incarnation? If we consider the martyrs, their glorification is admittedly more perfect than the sufferings by which they earn their salvation. This is because their glorification is identified with the moment when they are made perfect by possessing the beatific vision of God. Jesus Christ, however, is "full of grace and truth" (Jn. 1:14) from the first instant of His conception. Contrary to the new theology, His passage from death to resurrection does not signify a change of state bringing Him to His ultimate goal. This passage signifies rather the definitive extension of His glory to those parts of His being which were glorified only momentarily on Mount Thabor. The most important act of the life of Christ was, therefore, His obedience unto death by which He merited in a new way what He had previously merited from the first moment of His earthly existence: the glorification of His physical body and the sanctification unto glory of His mystical Body.

III. THE MASS AS A SACRIFICE

95. Classic theology and the new theology also disagree profoundly on the question of the sacrificial aspect of the Mass. In accordance with the Council of Trent and its definitions,[106] classic theology thinks of the Mass as a sacrificial action in its own right. Since sacrifice belongs to the *genus* of oblation, and since it is distinguished from other oblations by the destruction or immolation of the offering, theologians try to show how the "unbloody immolation" spoken of by the Council of Trent comes about in the rite of Mass.[107] The various approved opinions received the official recognition of Pope Pius XII in the encyclical *Mediator Dei*. Having restated the dogma,[108] the Pope explains what was contained, though not clarified, in the Council of Trent: at the altar, there is an unbloody immolation *per externa signa quae sunt mortis indices*, "by external signs which are symbols of His death. For by the 'transubstantiation' of bread into the Body of Christ and of wine into His Blood, His Body and Blood are both really present: now the Eucharistic species under which He is present symbolize the actual separation of His Body and Blood (...*cruentam corporis et sanguinis separationem figurant)*."[109] Pius XII shows that the sacrifice of the Mass is a memorial *insofar as it represents* the death of the Cross: "Thus the commemorative representation of His death, which actually took place on Calvary, is repeated in every Sacrifice of the altar, seeing that Jesus Christ is symbolically shown by separate symbols (*per distinctos indices*) to be in a state of victimhood."[110]

---

[106] DS 1751 (Dz. 948), Can. 1: If anyone says that in the Mass a true and real sacrifice is not offered to God, or that the act of offering is nothing else than Christ being given to us to eat: let him be anathema.

[107] DS 1743 (Dz. 940): [I]n this divine sacrifice, which is celebrated in the Mass, that same Christ is contained and immolated in an unbloody manner, who on the altar of the Cross "once offered Himself" in a bloody manner...

[108] DS 3847 (Dz. 2299): *Altaris sacrificium non mera est ac simplex Jesu Christi cruciatuum ac mortis commemoratio, sed vera ac propria sacrificatio*—The august Sacrifice of the altar, then, is no mere empty commemoration of the passion and death of Jesus Christ, but a true and proper act of sacrifice. (Daughters of St. Paul Edition, §68).

[109] DS 3848. Quoted from the Daughters of St. Paul edition, §70. The French version of the *Enchiridion* has unfortunately omitted the translation of the word *cruentam* [as has the English].

[110] *Ibid.*

96. The new theology abandons this teaching: "One cannot say that the bread separated from the wine is the sign of sacrifice (a sign of the separation of the body and blood and so of death). Thus understood, the death of Christ would be present only as a sign and not in reality."[111] More seriously, the new theology blames its medieval counterpart for no longer understanding the profundity of the sacramental mysteries, and for having thus reduced the sacrificial dimension of the Mass from the level of mystery to the level of signs:

> The expressions: "exemplary" sacrifice, sacrifice "*in figura*," "in image," "in mystery," "in sacrament," "in symbol," which expressed for the Fathers a particular mode of being of Christ's sacrifice, acquired [in the Middle Ages] a much more exterior meaning. It is, henceforth, clear that for the scholastic theologians, the sacrifice is purely in the exterior sign.[112]

For the new theology, the sacrifice is not found in the exterior rite but in the re-presentative role of the memorial: "Since the Passion was the sacrifice of Christ, the sacramental representation of the Passion is also the sacrifice of Christ since the mystery contains within itself the reality of the thing which is signified."[113] "The Mass is not, therefore, a sacrifice of its own nature, but is identical to the sacrifice of the Cross because it is its memorial; its sacrificial character consequently depends upon its nature as a memorial; it is essentially a sacrifice insofar as it is a memorial."[114] This brings us back to the essence of the doctrine of mysteries. By the memorial, the actions of salvation are really brought into the present moment, they are the content and proper object of the sacraments, and they constitute the inner reality of the mysteries of the liturgy: "The mystery [of worship] is not the individual application of graces which come from salvation wrought *historically* by Christ; it is rather the reality of the work of salvation in a sacramental mode. The effects [of salvation] spring from this very reality."[115] For,

---

[111] Salvatore Marsili, *I segni del misterio di Cristo*, (Rome: Edizioni Litugiche), 1987, p.290.

[112] Salvatore Marsili, *op. cit.*, pp.254, 259.

[113] Odo Casel, *Faites ceci en mémoire de moi*, p.165.

[114] Odo Casel, JLW, VIII, p.176.

[115] *Ibid.*, p.123.

Christian liturgy not only recalls the events that saved us but actualizes them, makes them present. The Paschal mystery of Christ is celebrated, not repeated. It is the celebrations that are repeated, and in each celebration there is an outpouring of the Holy Spirit that makes the unique mystery present (CCC §1104).

97. We can justifiably summarize the differences between classic theology and the new theology by the interpretation each gives to the verb *repraesentare*, used by the Council of Trent.[116] The new theology understands it as "making really present," and this happens through the objective dimension of the memorial. The Mass is then firstly a memorial (CCC §1362); it is only a sacrifice secondarily, and only then insofar as it is a memorial (CCC §1365); not because the Mass is a true, ritual sacrifice but because the memorial "makes the sacrifice of the Cross present" (§1366) beneath the veil of mystery. Classic theology, however, interprets *repraesentare* as "to represent or signify," *i.e.,* the role proper to an image in relation to the reality to which it refers. The Mass is then firstly a true, ritual sacrifice, but which has a memorial dimension insofar as it is an image representing the sacrifice of the Cross: "...the celebration of this sacrament is an image representing Christ's Passion."[117] If there is a true sacrifice and not simply the sign of a sacrifice—*sacramentum tantum*—it results not from the objectivity of the memorial, but from transubstantiation which makes the body and blood of the Divine Victim really present—the *res et sacramentum*. For various reasons which eventually all converge, the new theology increasingly empties the classic conception of the Eucharistic sacrifice by maintaining that the sacrifice of Christ cannot consist of His death alone, but must necessarily include His Resurrection and Ascension: "The sacrifice of Jesus cannot be understood as being limited to his death

---

[116] DS 1740: "*visibile...sacrificium, quo cruentum illud semel in cruce peragendum repraesentaretur...*"

[117] St. Thomas, *Summa Theologica*, III, Q. 83, A. 1 (*cf.* especially ad 2). In "*Le sacrifice de la messe selon Saint Thomas*" Angelicum, XV, Rome 1938, pp.262-85, Adolf Hoffmann shows definitively that St. Thomas does not understand *repraesentare* in the way the theologians of the Paschal mystery do. J. A. Sayés admits as much (*El misterio eucaristico*, BAC, 1986, p.283) when quoting from this work.

alone: his glorification is an essential part of it."[118] Consequently, the separate consecration of the sacred species is incapable alone of signifying the sacrifice of Christ since it only refers to His death and not to His Resurrection or Ascension. According to the new theology, this classic conception ought to give way to the memorial sacrifice which includes all of the mysteries of salvation. Thus by the theology of mysteries, "the emphasis falls again on the unicity of the saving action of the sacrifice of the Cross, excluding any subsequent sacrifices of a truly expiatory nature."[119]

98. A reciprocal exclusion of the theology of mysteries appears in the encyclical *Mediator Dei*. Some commentators tried at first to interpret the document as an approbation of this doctrine[120] while others claimed that the theology of mysteries had been ignored.[121] The evidence, however, was finally too compelling[122] and Pius XII's firm rejection of the new theology's explanations had to be recognized:

- The encyclical rejects the explanations of the new theology concerning the presence of the mysteries: "...these mysteries surely are present and operate continuously not in that uncertain and obscure manner about which certain more recent writers babble, but in the manner that is taught us by the Church."[123]
- The encyclical gives a classic explanation of the sacrificial nature of the Mass using language which is incompatible with the new doctrine. This doctrine does not countenance the possibility of saying that the Mass renews the

---

[118] J. A. Sayés, *El misterio eucaristico*, p.32. *Cf.* Salvatore Marsili, *I segni del miserio di Cristo*, p.290; Eugene Masure, *Le Sacrifice du Chef,* 7th ed. (Paris: Beauchesne, 1944), p.187; Odo Casel, *Faites ceci en mémoire de moi*, pp.172-73.

[119] Burkhard Neunheuser, article "*Memoriale,*" NDL, p.780.

[120] Jean Hild, "L'encyclique *Mediator Dei* et le movement de Maria-Laach," LMD, 67, 3rd Trimester, 1948, p.19.

[121] Jean Gaillard, "*Le mystère pascal dans le renouveau liturgique,*" LMD 67, 3rd Trimester 1961, p.33.

[122] Burkhard Neunheuser, article "*Misterio,*" NDL, p.814.

[123] DS 3855. *Cf.* Letter of the Holy Office to the Archbishop of Salzburg of Nov. 25, 1948.

sacrifice of the Cross: "The fact that the encyclical uses the word 'renew' (*iteratur*) when it states that the immolation of Calvary is repeated on the altar, makes us wonder whether we must await the next papacy for a total clarification of terms."[124] Moreover, the encyclical uses the word *demonstratio* (action of showing: DS 3848) and not Trent's expression *repraesentare* (DS 1740) because this word, interpreted in the sense of re-presenting or making present, had become the cornerstone of the theology of mysteries. For *Mediator Dei*, the Mass is not a sacrifice by virtue of being a memorial which makes the sacrifice of Calvary present. The Mass is a sacrifice because at the end of the double consecration a true, ritual, unbloody sacrifice (*per externa signa*, DS 3848), itself a sign of the bloody immolation (*significatur atque ostenditur*), is brought about.

99. Can the opposition between classic theology and the new theology perhaps be looked upon as a simple quarrel between schools of thought? Does this quarrel show a theological development which, by going beyond a confrontation that really belongs to the 16th century, could favor ecumenical relations with both Protestants and Jews while maintaining all the while the teaching of Trent? Such is the position that some people believe they can maintain:

> From its first appearance in the Old Testament and especially in the New Testament, the word and concept of memorial is so dense and full of meaning that when it is applied to the eucharistic celebration, it expresses "in some way" the presence of the commemorated reality, its "objective actualization," its presence *hic et nunc*. Such being the nature of the memorial and the sacrifice of Christ present in it, the statements made by the Council of Trent to defend Catholic doctrine remain valid....This conception of the Eucharist as a memorial in the fullest sense of the term...is of great importance for ecumenical dialogue.[125]

---

[124] J.A Sayés, *El misterio eucaristico*, BAC, 1986, p.316. Note incidentally the way in which Sayés falsifies the sense of the encyclical where it says, "The memorial presentation of his death which really happened on Calvary is renewed in the various sacrifices of the altar" (DS 3848). According to Pius XII, the Mass (*sacrificiis altaris*) is "*iterata*" and not the death of Christ.

In Part Three, a close examination of the teaching of the Council of Trent will enable us to judge the doctrinal value of this new explanation.

---

[125] Burkhard Neunheuser, article "*Memoriale*," NDL, pp.777, 779.

PART THREE

DOES THE LITURGICAL REFORM CONSTITUTE A DOGMATIC RUPTURE WITH TRADITION?

THESIS

100. The scope of the liturgical rupture that followed upon the revision of the missal by Pope Paul VI (Part One) has obliged us to set forth systematically the theological principles that guided the reform (Part Two). As the numerous official texts cited show, the theology of the Paschal mystery is essential to understanding the liturgical reform; indeed, it is inseparable from it, for the modern liturgy is the expression and the vector, so to speak, of the new theology.

- Because the theology of the Paschal mystery holds that there is no debt to be paid in order to satisfy divine justice offended by sin (*cf.* above, §§49-53), the propitiatory aspect of the Mass has been effaced from the new missal (§§ 35-48).

- Because the theology of the Paschal mystery no longer considers the redemptive act as the satisfaction offered by Christ to divine justice, but rather as the ultimate revelation of the eternal Covenant that God made with man (§§54-57), the structure of the rite of the new missal is that of a memorial meal that celebrates, makes present, and proclaims the divine Covenant (§§83-88), and not that of a sacrifice (§§4-13).

- Because the theology of the Paschal mystery no longer considers the Eucharist as a visible sacrifice, but rather as a symbol making mysteriously present the death and resurrection of the Lord and allowing, by means of these actions, a certain contact with Christ in glory (§§66-68, 89-90), the place of Christ Priest and Victim in the liturgy has been given over to the *Kyrios* who communicates Himself to the assembly (§§15-34).

101. Recognizing the indissoluble link between the new missal and the new theology of the Paschal mystery changes the nature of the judgment that needs to be made about the liturgical reform. Rather than being pastoral or even liturgical, it must be first and foremost doctrinal: Does the opposition shown in Parts One and Two between the theology of the Paschal mystery and classical theology merely represent two systems of thought which, though incompatible, are each capable of giving an adequate explanation of the Catholic Faith, or does this contradiction represent a calling into question of the Catholic Faith? On the answer to this question, which it is necessary to resolve, depends the attitude which the Catholic must adopt towards the liturgical reform.

102. Unfortunately, by juxtaposing the theology of the Paschal mystery with the teaching of the Council of Trent, we are obliged to conclude that the theses of the theology of the Paschal mystery are either dangerous for the faith, or else they directly challenge it on a major point, or else they openly contradict it.

- By affirming that Christ did not die on the Cross in order to satisfy the debt of punishment demanded by divine justice offended by sin, the theology of the Paschal mystery openly contradicts a truth of the Catholic Faith taught as such by the Council of Trent (Chapter 1).
- By making the sacrificial aspect of the Mass flow from the memorial dimension of the Mass, the theology of the Paschal mystery calls into question the teaching of the Council of Trent in this area. Despite its explanations, it does not seem to escape the condemnations pronounced by this Council (Chapter 2).
- Finally, by relying upon a new concept of sacrament, the theology of the Paschal mystery shows itself to be very dangerous to the Catholic Faith. By favoring heterodox theses on more than one point, this theology shows itself to belong to the modernist theology condemned by Pope St. Pius X (Chapter 3).

CHAPTER 1

A TRUTH OF
FAITH REFUSED

103. The reality of the vicarious satisfaction for sin made by Christ cannot be an object of discussion among Catholic theologians because it is a truth contained in the deposit of Revelation, and it has been sufficiently proposed for belief by the Church's Magisterium. If the word *satisfaction* does not occur in Sacred Scripture, it was used to express in precise language what Scripture meant by the word Redemption. When the Church had to refute the heresies of Protestantism concerning justification, she unhesitatingly employed this word to defend the dogma: "The meritorious cause is His most beloved only-begotten Son, our Lord Jesus Christ, 'who when we were enemies' [Eph. 1:13*ff*.], 'for the exceeding charity wherewith he loved us' [Eph. 2:4], merited justification for us by His most holy passion on the wood of the Cross, and made satisfaction for us to God the Father."[126] To defend the propitiatory end of the Mass against the same heresy, the infallible Magisterium declared: "If anyone says [of] the sacrifice of the Mass...that it ought not to be offered for the living and the dead, for sins, punishments, satisfactions, and other necessities: let him be anathema."[127] That is why it is necessary to conclude that "the merit and satisfaction of Christ cover more than the theories of theological schools or received theses. The fundamental idea conveyed by these terms belongs to the formula of the Catholic Faith used to express the work of supernatural Redemption eminently effected by the sacrifice of the Cross."[128]

---

[126] Council of Trent, Session 6, Decree on Justification, Chapter 7, DS 1529 (Dz. 799).

[127] Council of Trent, Session 22, On the Most Holy Sacrifice of the Mass, Canon 3, DS 1753 (Dz. 950).

[128] Jean Rivière, "Rédemption," *Dictionnaire de théologie catholique* (Letouzey et Ané, 1937), Vol. 13, col. 1920.

104. One cannot give a different meaning to the expressions employed by the popes and the councils (see above §53). Certainly, the Fathers of the Council of Trent did not deem it necessary to define the meaning of the word *satisfaction*, or what they meant by the satisfaction of Christ: a centuries-old doctrinal tradition guaranteed the exact meaning of these expressions. Were it necessary to give an authorized interpretation of the terms employed at Trent, we would find it in the Roman catechism published in the wake of the said Council: "…theologians make use of the word *satisfaction* to signify the compensation man makes, by offering to God some reparation for the sins he has committed….The first and highest degree of satisfaction is that by which whatever we owe to God on account of our sins is paid abundantly, even though He should deal with us according to the strictest rigor of His justice. This degree of satisfaction appeases God and renders Him propitious to us; and it is a satisfaction for which we are indebted to Christ our Lord alone, who paid the price of our sins on the cross, and offered to God a superabundant satisfaction."[129] The same Catechism explains elsewhere: "…the satisfaction which Jesus Christ has in an admirable manner made to God the Father for our sins is full and complete. The price which He paid for our ransom was not only adequate and equal to our debts, but far exceeded them…for when offered by His Son on the altar of the cross, it entirely appeased the wrath and indignation of the Father."[130]

105. While the work of our redemption can be considered from a number of aspects, the dogma of the vicarious satisfaction of Christ is so central to understanding the mystery that it can never be passed over or ignored. That is why the Magisterium of the Church has always defended it against attacks. Thus, to counter the liberal Protestantism of the 19th century that put in doubt this doctrine of Faith, Vatican I had prepared two condemnatory canons: "If anyone shall deny that the Word of God himself, by suffering and dying in the flesh that He assumed, has truly and properly offered satisfaction to God for our sins, and thus merited for us grace and glory; or if he shall dare affirm that the

---

[129] *Catechism of the Council of Trent*, Part 2, Ch. 24, p.296.
[130] *Ibid.*, p.60.

vicarious satisfaction, that is to say, the satisfaction offered by the unique Mediator for all men, is repugnant to the justice of God: let him be anathema."[131] The interruption of the Council prevented these canons from being published. The modernists and the new theologians profited from this to introduce the theses of liberal Protestantism into the Church. Pius XII denounced once again the error: "…without consideration of the definitions of the Council of Trent…the notion of sin in general as an offense against God [is perverted], and likewise the concept of the satisfaction made by Christ for us."[132] The preparatory schemas of Vatican II had also dedicated a chapter to the question of Christ's satisfaction, the last one of the dogmatic constitution *De deposito fidei pure custodiendo*. The purpose was clearly announced:

> The Church, born from the side of the second Adam, who on the Cross was, as it were, asleep, cannot tolerate that this mystery of our salvation be defiled by doctrinal corruptions. Because of the errors being spread today, and in order not to fail in her duty as Mother and Mistress, she affirms with especial vigor a truth that merits to be set among the principal truths of our religion, namely, the expiatory value of the death of Christ; and she declares that the Word of God, by suffering and dying in the human nature that He had assumed, has truly and properly satisfied for our sins.[133]

It then briefly sets forth in a clear and authoritative manner the three doctrinal points rejected by the new theology of the Paschal mystery:

> *[1]* Sin, according to the oracles of the Holy Ghost, is an iniquity and an injustice committed against God; for the sinner, by violating the divine law, sins in the presence of God, scorns Him, attacks the divine majesty, and becomes the enemy of God. *[2]* That is why [Scripture] also teaches us that our iniquities separate us from God, cry to Him for vengeance, make men the debtors of God, sons of wrath in need of the gratuitous mercy of God in order to be reconciled with Him. *[3]* To repair the

---

[131] Schema of a constitution, *De praecipuis mysteriis fidei*, IV, p.3.

[132] Pope Pius XII, *Humani Generis,* DS 3891 (Dz. 2318).

[133] Schema constitutionis dogmaticae *De deposito fidei pure custodiendo,* in *Sacrosanctum oecumenicum Concilium vaticanum secundum: schemata constitutionum et decretorum, de quibus disceptabitur in Concilii sessionibus,* series prima, Typis Polyglottis Vaticanis, 1962, C. X, No. 53, p.65.

injustice caused to the divine majesty, the Son of God in person offered to the eternal Father His own blood by the Holy Ghost, and reconciled us to God by His death.[134]

By refusing to consider that the Redemption includes the act by which Christ paid to God the entire debt of pain incurred by our sins (the doctrine of vicarious satisfaction), the theology of the Paschal mystery sets itself in opposition to a truth of the Catholic Faith.

---

[134] *Ibid.*

CHAPTER 2

A TRUTH OF FAITH
PUT IN DOUBT

106. The Fathers of the Council of Trent addressed the sacrificial character of the Mass by taking as their point of departure a résumé in ten articles of the doctrines of Luther, Melanchton, and Calvin. The first point affirmed that "the Mass is neither a sacrifice nor an oblation for sin, but only a commemoration of the sacrifice of the Cross; the Fathers called it a sacrifice in the metaphorical sense, for it is not a sacrifice in the true and strict sense of the word, but only as a testament and a promise of the remission of sins."[135] Confronted by this error, the Council of Trent defined what the Mass is, and the three aspects by which it is in relation with the sacrifice of Calvary.

- The Mass is a sacrifice in the proper sense of the term, real and visible,[136]
- that represents, commemorates and applies the sacrifice of the Cross,[137]
- and not merely a commemoration.[138]

107. Since then, the sacrificial character of the Mass has stood as a wall of separation between Protestants and Catholics: the former affirm that the Mass is a memorial meal of the sacrifice

---

[135] *Concilium Tridentinum*, (Fribourg: Ed. Gorresiana, 1910), Tome VII, Vol. 1, p.375.

[136] DS 1740 (Dz. 938): "Christ…so that He might leave to His beloved spouse the Church a visible sacrifice (as the nature of man demands)…"; DS 1751 (Dz. 948): "If anyone says that in the Mass a true and real sacrifice is not offered to God,…: let him be anathema."

[137] DS1740 (Dz. 938): "…[leave a visible sacrifice] whereby that bloody sacrifice once to be completed on the Cross might be represented, and the memory of it remain even to the end of the world and its saving grace be applied to the remission of those sins which we daily commit…"

[138] DS 1753 (Dz. 950): "If anyone says that the sacrifice of the Mass is … a mere commemoration (*nudam commemorationem*) of the sacrifice consummated on the Cross…: let him be anathema."

of the Cross and not a true sacrifice, while the latter hold that it is truly a sacrifice and not a mere memorial. The theology of the Paschal mystery seemed to provide a path to reconcile the two by explaining that the Mass, while being a memorial meal, can nonetheless be called a true sacrifice because it is an *objective* memorial: "Because it is the memorial of Christ's Passover, *the Eucharist is also a sacrifice*" (CCC §1365). It seemed that it would be possible to retain the Tridentine declaration on the triple relation between the Eucharist and the Cross: "The Eucharist is thus a sacrifice because it *re-presents* (makes present) the sacrifice of the cross, because it is its *memorial* and because it *applies* its fruit" (CCC §1366). Yet this interpretation of the Council of Trent's definitions raises some questions:

- Did the Council of Trent understand the word *repraesentatur* in this manner?
- Does this manner of "making present" suffice to allow the term *sacrifice* to be applied to the Mass truly and properly?
- The answer to these two questions makes it seem to us that the thesis of the Paschal mystery does not avoid the qualifier "*nuda commemoratio*."

I. THE MASS, A VISIBLE SACRIFICE

108. While it is true that *repraesentare* signifies "to make present," nevertheless to understand what it means, it is necessary to make certain distinctions. A thing can be said to be present in several ways: by its actual presence, by its operation, or by an image that resembles it. It is necessary to determine in what sense the Council of Trent uses this word. Certainly, it holds that the sacrifice of the Cross is present by its action (second sense), but designates this reality by the word *applicare*, using it a few lines later. By the verb *repraesentare*, it means that the Mass is a certain image that represents the bloody sacrifice of the Cross (third meaning). Both the text and the context impose this interpretation of the word's meaning.

109. The text of the Council imposes this interpretation; it explains that, in fact, it is by the *visible* sacrifice—a visibility necessitated by human nature—that the bloody sacrifice is represented. Now, what is visible in the Mass are the Eucharistic symbols, that is, the species of bread and wine. Their separate consecration serves as a symbolic rite, as a representative image of the sacrifice of the Cross. At the Mass, Christ is "immolated under visible signs."[139] Moreover, if the conciliar text recognizes a certain continuity between the rite of the ancient Passover and that instituted by Christ, it is as a reminder that the ancient Passover was not only social, but also properly sacrificial. That is why the visible rite of the Eucharist must be sacrificial:

> For, after He had celebrated the ancient feast of the Passover, which the multitude of the children of Israel sacrificed in memory of their exodus from Egypt, He instituted a new Passover, Himself to be immolated under visible signs by the Church through the priests, in memory of His own passage from this world to the Father....[140]

Finally, the Fathers of Trent cite the tenth chapter of the First Epistle to the Corinthians (DS 1742). This passage supports the sacrificial character of the rite of the Mass: St. Paul speaks about the Christian altar as opposed to the altars of the pagans, where idolatrous sacrifices are immolated.

110. This interpretation is confirmed by the sources cited by the Council of Trent: The Council of Florence had already employed the term in this sense when speaking of the offerings, stating that the water mingled with wine represented the blood and the water that flowed from Christ's side.[141]

It is well known that the Fathers of the Council of Trent gave a pre-eminent place to the works of St. Thomas Aquinas.[142] Thus, to the implicit question: "How is the Mass the sacrifice of Christ, if Christ was only offered once (Heb. 9:28)? Trent answers: "Because it represents it and applies it," a reply drawn from the *Summa Theologica*.[143] In this passage there is no doubt possible as to

---

[139] DS 1741 (Dz. 938).

[140] *Ibid.*

[141] DS 1320 (Dz. 698).

[142] "The *Summa Theologica* merited the signal honor of being placed on the altar next to the Bible...." Jacques-Marie (Santiago) Ramirez, *Introduction à saint Thomas d'Aquin*, BAC, (1975), p.189.

the meaning St. Thomas gives to the word *repraesentatio*: "The celebration of this sacrament is an image representing Christ's Passion, in which His blood was separated from His body."

111. The sacrificial character of the rites of the Mass is, thus, clearly affirmed by the Council of Trent. That is why the Roman Catechism rightly says: "All [of the many solemn rites and ceremonies] tend to display the majesty of this august Sacrifice...."[144] There remains one question to put to the theologians of the Paschal mystery: if the Mass is only a sacrifice insofar as it is contained under the veil of the mystery, how can they claim to adhere to the teaching of the Council of Trent, which characterizes this sacrifice as "visible"?

II. THE MASS, A SACRIFICE "*VERE ET PROPRIE*"

112. The Council of Trent teaches not only that the Mass is the image of the sacrifice of the Cross, but also that it is truly and properly a sacrifice. Strictly speaking, there can only be a true and proper sacrifice where there is a true victim and real immolation. It is in this sense that the Catholic Church designates the Mass as a sacrifice. Through transubstantiation, the sacred species are not only a symbol of Christ immolated, but the very same victim immolated on the Cross; and there is not only a figure of immolation, but real separation, albeit unbloody, of the body and blood of our Lord. The theology of the Paschal mystery leaves aside these explanations, preferring to say that the Mass is a sacrifice because, insofar as it is an objective memorial (making present "*in mysterio*") of the Passion and of the Resurrection, it truly contains the sacrifice of Christ. But such an explanation does not correspond to the affirmation of the Council of Trent that the Mass is a sacrifice *vere et proprie*. For, to designate the container (the rite of the Mass) by one of the things contained (the sacrifice of the Cross), or the whole (the Eucharist) by one of its parts (that which is contained under the veil of the mystery), is to use a literary de-

---

[143] St. Thomas Aquinas, *Summa Theologica*, III, Q. 83, A. 1.
[144] *Catechism of the Council of Trent*, p.259.

vice which, however authorized, has the effect of taking away the literal meaning of the thing so named.

III. "*NUDA COMMEMORATIO*"?

113. By affirming the objective character of the memorial, the theology of the Paschal mystery would seem to distinguish itself from those theologies which reduce the Mass to a "*nuda commemoratio*" of the sacrifice of the Cross, and thus escape Trent's anathema: "It is a real memorial, and not only a mental memorial, a purely conceptual reminder, a '*nuda commemoratio*' as the Council of Trent calls it when opposing Luther's doctrine."[145] Yet, when the Fathers of Trent defined the Mass as a true sacrifice, they not only intended to denounce a simple subjective memorial, but also the assimilation of the Mass to a sacrifice in the figurative sense of the word. The condemnation, as we know, was directed against the following proposition: "[The Mass] is only a commemoration of the sacrifice of the Cross; the Fathers called it a sacrifice in a metaphorical sense, for it is not a sacrifice in the true and proper sense of the word."[146] Now, whether the memorial is objective or subjective, it is always in a figurative manner that it will be called a sacrifice. Despite its denials, the theology of the Paschal mystery seems, then, to incur on this point the condemnation of the Council of Trent.

By considering the Mass as a sacrifice only insofar as it is a memorial which contains "*in mysterio*" the sacrifice of the Cross, the theology of the Paschal mystery weakens the visibility of the sacrifice as taught by the Church, and can no longer "*vere et proprie*" designate the Mass as a sacrifice. This cannot do justice to a truth of Faith, and seems thereby to incur the condemnation pronounced by the Council of Trent as regards the "*nuda commemoratio.*"

---

[145] Burkhard Neunheuser, "*Memoriale*," NDL, p.777.
[146] *Concilium Tridentinum*, ed. Gorresiana, (Fribourg, 1910), Tome VII, Vol. 1, p.375.

CHAPTER 3

A DANGER FOR
THE FAITH

114. As we have said, one of the main keys to understanding the theology of the Paschal mystery is the meaning that it gives the word *sacrament*. Because it considers a sacrament as a reality that makes present the divine (the "mystery" properly so-called) beneath the veils of the symbol (the "sacrament"), it conceives of the sacrament as the arena where the experience of the meeting with God can take place. "Sign and means of intimate union with God" (*Lumen Gentium* §1), the new notion of sacrament, centered as it is on the symbol and on the divine made accessible to human experience, is applied to a whole range of objects in a way hitherto unknown. Yet can this teaching properly express the Church's teaching both in the domain of the sacraments and in other branches of theology where it is applied. It seems that, on the contrary, by diluting the teaching of the Church, it is the source of numerous errors.

115. Because it considers the whole body of the liturgy (the "mystery of worship") as a sacrament, the new theology cannot adopt the capital distinction which the Church has always made when treating of the seven sacraments: the properly sacramental act works *ex opere operato* (DS 1608), whereas the secondary rites derive their efficacy both from the action of the Church which accompanies them and from the dispositions of the faithful who receive them, *ex opere operantis* (DS 3844). This distinction maintains a point of faith by which the sacraments are truly causes of grace,[147] instrumental causes,[148] as the recipient's faith does not affect the causality of the sacrament, though his habitual disposition may affect the result. For its part, the new theology advances a new conception of sacramental efficacy. If by "the very fact of the action's being performed" one no longer understands the sac-

---

[147] DS 1310 (Dz. 695).
[148] DS 1529 (Dz. 799).

ramental action which, each time, is accomplished and applied to the soul, but rather the very action of Christ accomplished once for all (CCC §1128) and present under the veil of the mystery, it seems necessary to affirm that the sacraments, in order to be efficacious ("*ex opere operato*") require that the symbols, making present the actions of Christ, be interpreted by the faith of the recipient in order to establish contact with the saving action of Christ: "…to receive in faith the gift of his Eucharist is to receive the Lord himself."[149] Hence we are entitled to wonder if such a conception, which subordinates the efficacy of the sacrament to the act of faith which interprets the symbol, does not amount to an implicit denial of the teaching of Trent. Moreover, by the novelty of calling the sacraments, sacraments of the faith, by explaining their finality principally by the way they are known and no longer by their salutary effect upon the soul, and by assimilating to them the liturgy taken as a whole, this theology dangerously skirts the anathema which the Council of Trent attributed to those for whom the sacraments have been instituted for no other purpose than for "the nourishing of faith alone."[150]

116. Because they consider the sacrament as the making present the divine under the veils of the symbol, many contemporary theologians invalidate one of the points of the teaching of the Council of Trent on the Real Presence. This Council affirms that the holy Eucharist contains truly, really and substantially, and not merely "as by a sign or figure" the body and blood of our Lord united to His soul and His divinity. But with the symbolic "screen" of the new theology, is such a distinction still necessary? Forsaking the distinction between *substance* and *accident* which is considered too scholastic by the new theology, but which was used by the Council of Trent,[151] the new theology, because it adopts the new modern concepts of *phenomenon* and *foundation,* will naturally recognize the presence of the body and blood in itself (*substantia*) by making it depend upon the interpretation it will be given by the man to whom it appears ("*in symbolo*") as

---

[149] CCC §1336.
[150] DS 1605 (Dz. 848).
[151] DS 1640-42 (Dz. 876-77).

bread and wine. In the Old Testament the believer saw beneath the symbol of bread and wine "the fruit of the promised land, the pledge of God's faithfulness to his promises." In the same symbol reinterpreted by Jesus in the New Testament, the faith now discovers the body of Christ, a new fundamental reality.[152] It is easy to see how such a theology could give rise to theses such as transignification, transfinalization, *etc.*, which have been cropping up in theology departments[153] and catechism instructions.[154]

117. By extending its notion of "sacrament" to other branches of theology, the new theology multiplies the problems and the sources of error. By considering Christ as the sacrament of the divinity, it runs the risk of abandoning the notion of His personal unity, since a sign, in order to stand in relation to the thing signified, must be a distinct and separate entity from it. This is the source of the numerous errors in Christology which have spread and continue to spread. Likewise, by applying this conception to the Church (*Lumen Gentium* §1), it succeeds in dividing the quasi-personal union that the Church maintains with Christ. The new theology distinguishes the Church of Christ ("mystery") from the Catholic Church ("sacrament"), the latter being contained by the former without being identical, or limited, to it. Hence the explicit rejection of the teaching of *Mystici Corporis*, according to which the Catholic Church *is* the unique Mystical Body of Christ.[155] This is the acknowledged source[156] of an ecumenical pastoral teaching condemned beforehand.

118. This conception of a sacrament, which is supposed to be a reality that makes present the divine under the veils of the symbol in order to allow the experience of the divine, is not only dangerous for the Faith, but even incurs the condemnation that Pope

---

[152] CCC §1334.

[153] *Cf.* For example, *L'eucharistie et le sens des sacrements, Faculté de théologie de Lyon* (1971) pp.62, 63.

[154] *Cf.* Arnaud de Lassus, *Le sacrifice de la messe dans la nouvelle catéchèse* (DMM, 1985), pp.41-48.

[155] *Cf.* Joseph Ratzinger, *"La pluralité des confessions ne relativise pas l'exigence de la vérité," Osservatore romano de langue française,* October 17, 2000, p.10.

[156] *Cf.* Joseph Ratzinger, *"L'ecclésiologie de la constitution conciliaire* Lumen Gentium," DC 2223, April 2, 2000, pp.310-11.

St. Pius X made of modernism in the encyclical letter *Pascendi Dominici Gregis.*[157] He therein already denounced this "theology based on the doctrine of experience and of symbolism." How is it possible not to recognize the new theology of the sacrament in the description made by St. Pius X of modernism, for which the formulae of the faith are like sacraments, *i.e.,* signs and means: "...but as far as faith is concerned, they [the formulae] are inadequate signs of its object, usually called *symbolae;* in their relationship to the believer, they are mere instruments"[158]; modernism, for which the sacraments are "mere symbols or signs, although not lacking efficacy....Surely they [the modernists] would speak more clearly if they affirm that the sacraments were instituted solely to nourish faith"[159]; modernism, for which the Word of God is like a "collection of experiences" capable of making the past and future actions of the Savior present, for "he who believes either, lives the past by recollection in the manner of the present, or the future by anticipation....Thus, then, in these Books God certainly speaks through the believer, but as the theology of the modernists puts it, only by *immanence* and *vital permanence.*"[160]

Insofar as it rests upon philosophies of the symbolic type, this notion of sacrament cannot be reconciled with the Church's doctrine on the sacraments. Because this notion corrupts the branches of theology where it is introduced, it is dangerous for the Faith.

---

[157] St. Pius X, *Pascendi Dominici Gregis*, AAS 40 (1907), pp.596-628.
[158] DS 3483 (Dz. 2079).
[159] DS 2089 (Dz. 2089).
[160] DS 3490 (Dz. 2090).

GENERAL CONCLUSION

119. We have not intended this study to be an exhaustive examination and exposition of the deficiencies and weaknesses of either the new missal or the theology of the Paschal mystery. In the liturgical domain, we could have developed more the influence and effects of false ecumenism on this reform, or highlighted the unreasonableness of concocting a liturgical rite by committee. With regard to the theology of the Paschal mystery, several serious doctrinal muddles would need to be clarified, if only in the domain of sacramental theology. We are thinking, in particular, of the way in which the institution of the sacraments by Christ is treated, and of the baneful consequences for the sacrament of Holy Orders that the new theology has brought about. Because of its intimate connection with the theology of the Paschal mystery, the liturgical reform is undoubtedly one of the major causes of the identity crisis which the Catholic priesthood is undergoing. It is not possible to alter the sacrifice of the Mass and its propitiatory end without at the same time undermining the priesthood, for "every high priest taken from among men is ordained for men in the things that appertain to God, that he may offer up gifts and sacrifices for sins" (Heb. 5:1).

120. Our intention has been rather to remain at the heart of the matter. The detailed analysis of the numerous and substantial liturgical modifications introduced into the Mass by the reform of Paul VI, then the comprehensive exposition of the theology of the Paschal mystery as it is presented by its promoters or official spokesmen, have made clear to us that the prime, guiding principle of the liturgical reform is "the accomplishing of the Paschal mystery of Christ in the liturgy of the Church," as Pope John Paul II said.[161] Because the theology of the Paschal mystery teaches that sin does not incur any debt of justice to be paid in reparation for the outrage to God's majesty, and consequently no longer considers the vicarious satisfaction of Christ as one of the essential elements of the redemptive act, the liturgical reform removed from

---

[161] Pope John Paul II, *Vicesimus Quintus Annus*, Dec. 4, 1988.

the rite of Mass everything referring to the pain due to sin, as well as to its propitiatory end. Because the theology of the Paschal mystery considers the Redemption as being only the ultimate manifestation of the eternal love of the Father for men, a shift in teaching occurs. Christ, who by His Incarnation entered into union with every man, responds to the Father's love by His Incarnation, and man in turn is invited to respond to the Father's love by faith in order to enter into contact with the glorious Christ made present under the veils of the mystery. Because the theology of the Paschal mystery considers that the memorial rite alone can make present the mysteries of the death and resurrection of Christ which are now past, the liturgical reform has profoundly modified the structure of the rite of Mass to the point of eliminating its properly sacrificial character.

121. Now, the infallible teaching of the Church, chiefly expressed in the texts of the Council of Trent, obliges us to consider the vicarious satisfaction of Christ as one of the principal truths of our Faith. This Council teaches that the Mass is "*vere et proprie*" a sacrifice, a visible sacrifice, a teaching which makes the emphasis placed by the theology of the Paschal mystery on the memorial aspect of the Mass unacceptable. Moreover, recent acts of the Magisterium have put us on guard against a "symbolic" theology that would only consider a sacrament insofar as it is a mystery, for such a theology would prove dangerous to the Faith. We must conclude that the theology of the Paschal mystery, insofar as it refuses the vicarious satisfaction of Christ, explicitly refuses a truth of Faith. Because this theology cannot subscribe to the dogmatic definitions relative to the sacrifice of the Mass, it calls into question a truth of Faith. This same theology, centered as it is on the notion of "mystery," ultimately proves to be dangerous to the Faith because it favors serious doctrinal deviations.

122. The doctrine of the Paschal mystery, with its serious doctrinal deficiencies, is, then, at origin of the liturgical reform. Certainly, the reformed missal does not deny Catholic dogma outright, but its authors have so oriented the gestures and the words, they have made such significant omissions and introduced numerous ambiguous expressions, and all in order to make the

rite conform to the theology of the Paschal mystery and to give expression to it. Consequently, the new missal no longer propagates the *lex credendi* of the Church, but rather a doctrine that smacks of heterodoxy. That is why one cannot say that the reformed rite of Mass of 1969 is "orthodox" in the etymological sense of the word: it does not offer "right praise" to God. Equally, one cannot say that the rite of Mass resulting from the reform of 1969 is that of the Church, even if it was conceived by churchmen.[162] And lastly, one cannot say that the new missal is for the faithful "the first and indispensable source of the true Christian spirit,"[163] where the Church "communicates in abundance the treasures of the *depositum fidei*, of the truth of Christ."[164] In light of these serious deficiencies, "the only attitude of fidelity to the Church and to Catholic doctrine appropriate for our salvation is a categorical refusal to accept this reformation."[165] In such a situation, we are therefore obliged to hold fast to the traditional liturgy, which is certainly worthy of God, which has never been abrogated,[166] and which has produced so many fruits of holiness down the ages. That is why, without any rebellion, bitterness or resentment on our part, but rather because we are persuaded that by so doing we cannot render greater service to the holy Catholic Church, to the Sovereign Pontiff and to future generations, we follow the adjuration that Archbishop Marcel Lefebvre, founder of the Priestly Society of Saint Pius X addressed to us on September 23, 1979:

> For the glory of the Most Blessed Trinity, for the love of Our Lord Jesus Christ, for the devotion to the Blessed Virgin Mary, for the love of the Church, for the love of the Pope, for the love of bishops, of priests, of all the faithful, for the salvation of the world, for the salvation of souls, keep this Testament of Our

---

[162] *Cf.* Canonical Annex *in fine.*

[163] St. Pius X, motu proprio *Tra le sollecitudini* of Nov. 22, 1903, in *Papal Teachings: The Liturgy,* selected and arranged by the Benedictine Monks of Solesmes, (French ed. Desclée, 1961), No. 220.

[164] Pope Pius XII, Allocution to the International Congress on Pastoral Liturgy, September 22, 1956, *op. cit.* No. 796.

[165] Marcel Lefebvre, Declaration of November 21, 1974, in *Un éveque parle,* 3rd. ed. (DMM, 1976) [translation cited from Michael Davies's *Apologia pro Marcel Lefebvre, p.40*].

[166] See the Appendix on the canonical status of the Tridentine Mass.

Lord Jesus Christ! Keep the Sacrifice of Our Lord Jesus Christ! Keep the Mass of All Time![167]

---

[167] Sermon of His Grace, the Most Reverend Archbishop Marcel Lefebvre on the Occasion of His Sacerdotal Jubilee, Sept. 23, 1979, Paris, France [quoted in full in Davies, *Apologia pro Marcel Lefebvre*, Vol. 2, (Angelus Press, 1983), p.343].

THE CANONICAL STATUS
OF THE TRIDENTINE MASS

CAN ONE IN GOOD CONSCIENCE USE
THE MISSAL REVISED BY POPE SAINT PIUS V?

Ever since the constitution *Missale Romanum* of April 3, 1969, was promulgated, the consequent legal status of the traditional Roman liturgy celebrated according to the missal revised by St. Pius V, the so-called Tridentine Mass, has been disputed.

When the matter is discussed, several documents in addition to the *Missale Romanum* are invariably cited: the instruction of the Sacred Congregation for Divine Worship dated October 20, 1969; Pope Paul VI's discourse of November 26, 1969; the new Instruction for the Sacred Congregation for Divine Worship dated June 14, 1971; a Notice by the aforementioned Congregation dated October 28, 1974; Pope Paul VI's Allocution to the Consistory of May 24, 1976; and, lastly, a letter emanating from the Sacred Congregation of Divine Worship addressed to the Bishop of Siena in 1999.

Based upon these documents, of varying authority and objectives, some claim to infer that Pope Paul VI's missal henceforth constitutes the liturgical common law in the Latin Church, while the possibility of celebrating Mass according to the Tridentine rite, which had acquired the status of a mere privilege, could eventually be allowed under certain conditions in the framework of the indult *Quattor Abhinc Annos* of October 3, 1984. Nonetheless, the commission of cardinals formed by Pope John Paul II in 1986 for the purpose of studying the application of the motu proprio *Quattor Abhinc Annos* unanimously judged that the Tridentine Mass had never been abrogated, and that no bishop was ever justified in forbidding a priest to use this missal.

Indeed, an attentive examination of the arguments adduced by those who defend the obligatory character of Paul VI's missal clearly shows the falsehood of their argumentation.

1. The Missal revised by St. Pius V was not abrogated.

According to Canon 20 of the *1983 Code of Canon Law*, a later law abrogates or derogates from an earlier law if it expressly so states. Now, the letter of the Sacred Congregation for the Divine Worship to the Bishop of Siena in 1999 acknowledges that "in the apostolic constitution *Missale Romanum,* no explicit formula of abrogation of the Roman missal so-called of St. Pius V occurs."

2. The Missal revised by St. Pius V was not "obrogated."

According to Canon 20 of the Code of Canon Law, a later law supersedes or, to use the technical word, "obrogates" an earlier law if it integrally reorders the whole subject matter of the earlier law, and supplants it. The letter of the Sacred Congregation for Divine Worship to the Bishop of Siena in 1999 seems to maintain that the Tridentine missal would have been suppressed by a form of obrogation. Its arguments, however, are not pertinent:

(a) This letter asserts in the first place that "if the will of the Pontiff had been to leave in force the preceding liturgical forms as an alternative that could be freely chosen, he should have said so explicitly." On the contrary, the Code of Canon Law declares that "laws which prescribe a penalty, or restrict the free exercise of rights, or contain an exception to the law, are to be interpreted strictly" (Canon 18); and that "in doubt, the revocation of a previous law is not presumed; rather, later laws are to be related to earlier ones and, as far as possible, harmonized with them" (Canon 21).

(b) This letter asserts that documents subsequent to the constitution *Missale Romanum* confirm the obligatory character of Paul VI's missal. But a mere papal discourse or an instruction from a Roman Congregation does not possess the authority necessary to make the missal obligatory when the apostolic constitution directly treating of the matter did not do so, since "a lower legislator cannot validly make a law which is contrary to that of a higher legislator" (Canon 135, §2; *cf.* Canons 33, §1 and 34, §2).

(c) This letter asserts that "usage" manifests the obligatory character of Paul VI's missal. Yet this usage has never been universal; quite the contrary, the persistent usage of the Tridentine missal is universally recognized, notwithstanding the persecutions and abuses of power by which some priests using this missal have been afflicted.

(d) This letter asserts that the obligatory character of Paul VI's missal can be seen by comparing it to the situation described in Canon 6, §1, No. 4 taken together with Canon 19. But if one were to reason by means of analogy, then it would also be necessary to suppose that the supreme legislator, acting with wisdom and equity as did his predecessor St. Pius V, did not desire to abrogate a liturgy hundreds of years old. Moreover, interpretation by analogy is used to compare a new law whose meaning is in doubt to previous similar laws. Yet the analogy being proposed compares a doubtful law of 1969 to a law promulgated in 1983, because Canon 6, §1, No. 4 treats of the relation between the *1983 Code of Canon Law* and previous disciplinary laws. Besides, if a tacit abrogation of the previous law were really envisioned, then it should have been compared to Canon 20 which, in fact, treats of tacit abrogation. Finally, this would be the first time that a pope had acted in such an important matter (abolishing a missal in usage for at least four centuries) without explicitly stating his intention.

3. The Missal revised by St. Pius V has acquired the status of an immemorial custom.

Long before it was prescribed by law, the usage of the Roman missal had given it the force of an immemorial custom; it had existed for long centuries before the bull *Quo Primum* promulgated by St. Pius V. Now, a law cannot revoke centennial or immemorial customs without making express mention of them (Canon 28). By its silence on this point, Pope Paul VI's apostolic constitution leaves intact this immemorial liturgical custom.

4. The Missal revised by St. Pius V is protected by an indult.

Moreover, St. Pius V granted in perpetuity to all priests a specific indult, conceding to them the tranquil enjoyment of the perpetual right to celebrate publicly and privately the rite which he had codified. This indult could not be suppressed without express mention, for "a universal law does not derogate from a particular or from a special law, unless the law expressly provides otherwise" (Canon 20). By its silence on this point, the apostolic constitution of Pope Paul VI leaves intact the privilege granted in perpetuity by St. Pius V.

5. Paul VI's Missal does not have the character of a true law.

Even if the canonical forms abrogating or obrogating the missal revised by St. Pius V had been perfectly respected; even if it were possible to abrogate an immemorial liturgical custom, protected as well by a specific, perpetual indult, the obligatory character of Pope Paul VI's missal would still not be established. "For an ordinance promulgated by a legislator to be a true law, obligatory for the community concerned, it is necessary by the nature of things that it be in itself and in relation to its object, right and just, possible to observe and truly useful to the commonweal. These qualities constitute the intrinsic reason for the existence of laws."[168] And yet, Paul VI's missal, by reason of its serious theological defects, contributes directly to the lessening of faith, of piety, and of religious practice, as experience shows daily. For this reason, it is neither right, nor just, nor helpful to the common good. Thus it does not have the character of a true law, and cannot be obligatory.

6. One can in good conscience use the Missal revised by St. Pius V.

The missal revised by St. Pius V was neither abrogated nor "obrogated" by the legislator: hence one can use it in good conscience as a liturgical law still in force.

---

[168] Michiels, *Normae generales juris canonici*, I (Lublin, 1929), p.486.

The missal revised by St. Pius V has the character of an immemorial custom, protected, moreover, by a specific, perpetual indult: for this reason, one can use it in good conscience.

The missal of Pope Paul VI, because of its serious theological defects, does not have and cannot have the character of a true and binding law. While waiting for the legislator to publish the necessary theological, liturgical, and canonical clarifications, one can in good conscience use the missal revised by St. Pius V.

BIBLIOGRAPHY

Bouyer, Louis. *Eucharistie*. Desclée, 1990. [English version tr. by C. U. Quinn. University of Notre Dame Press, 1968.]

Bouyer, Louis. *"Mysterion,"* in *Supplément de la Vie spirituelle,* No. 23, 1952.

Bouyer, Louis. *La vie de la liturgie. Lex orandi.* Paris: Cerf, 1956.

Bruylants, Placide. *Les oraisons du missel romain.* Mont-César, 1952.

Bugnini, Annibale. *La riforma liturgica.* Rome: Edizioni liturgiche, 1983.

Casel, Odo. *Faites ceci en mémoire de moi. Lex orandi.* Paris: Cerf, 1962.

Casel, Odo. *Le mystère du culte. Lex orandi.* Paris: Cerf, 1964.

Dalmais, Irénée-Henri. *Initiation à la liturgie. Cahiers de la Pierre-qui-vire.* Desclée, 1958.

Dalmais, Irénée-Henri. *"La liturgie, acte de l'Église."* LMD 19, 3rd Trimester, 1949.

De Jong, J. P. *L'Eucharistie comme réalité symbolique. Cogitatio fidei.* Cerf, 1972.

Faculté de théologie de Lyon. *L'Eucharistie et le sens des sacraments.* 1971.

Féret, Henri-Marie. *La messe, rassemblement de la communauté. Lex orandi.* Paris: Cerf, 1947.

Gaillard, Jean. *"La liturgie du mystère pascal."* LMD 67, 3rd Trimester, 1961.

Guardini, Romano. *Besinnung vor der Feier des hl. Messe.* Moguncia, 1939.

Hamman, Adalbert. *La Rédemption et l'histoire du monde.* Paris: Alsatia, 1947.

Hild, Jean. *"L'encyclique Mediator Dei et le mouvement de Maria-Laach."* LMD 14, 2nd. Trimester, 1948.

Hoffmann, Adolf. *"Le sacrifice de la messe selon saint Thomas."* Angelicum XV. Rome, 1938.

Jungmann, Joseph-André. *Missarum solemnia.* Aubier, 1951.

Lassus, Arnaud de. *Le sacrifice de la messe dans la nouvelle catéchèse.* DMM, 1985.

Le Brun, Pierre. *Explication de la messe. Lex orandi.* Paris: Cerf, 1949.

Lefebvre, Marcel. *Un Evêque parle,* DMM, 1976.

Marsili, Salvatore. *"La misa, misterio pascual y misterio de la Iglesia"* in *La sagrada liturgia.* Madrid: Studium, 1965.

Marsili, Salvatore. *I segni del misterio di Cristo.* Rome: *Edizioini Liturgiche,* 1987.

Martin Patino, J. M. *et al. Nuevas normas de la misa.* BAC, 1969.

Martimort, Aimé-Georges. *Les lignes essentielles de la messe. Lex orandi.* Paris: Cerf, 1947.

Masure, Eugene. *Le sacrifice du Chef.* Paris: Beauchesne, 1944.

Mersche, Emile. *Théologie du Corps mystique.* Paris: Desclée, 1949.

Montcheuil, Yves de. *Leçons sur le Christ.* Paris: Éd. de l'Épi, 1949.

Neunheuser, Burkhard, *"Memoriale."* NDL.

Neunheuser, Burkhard. *"Misterio."* NDL.

Nicolas, Jean-Hervé. *Synthèse dogmatique. De la Trinité à la Trinité.* Fribourg: *Éditions universitaires,* 1985.

Nocent, Adrien. *"Sobre la reforma del ordinario de la Misa"* in *La sagrada liturgia renovada por el Concilio.* Madrid: Studium, 1965.

Pinard, Henry de la Boullaye. *"Jésus rédempteur." Conférences de Notre-Dame de Paris.* Spes, 1936.

Pius X. Motu proprio *Tra le sollecitudini* (Nov. 22, 1903).

Ratzinger, Joseph. *Die sakramentale Bergrundung christlicher Existenz.* 7th ed. Freising: Ed. Kyrios, 1966.

Roguet, Aimon-Marie. *"Qu'est-ce que le mystère de la liturgie.* CNPL, 2000.

Roguet, Aimon-Marie. *"Qu'est-ce que le mystère pascal."* LMD 67, 3rd Trimester, 1969.

Richard, Louis. *Le mystère de la Rédemption.* Desclée, 1959.

Rivière, Jean. *Dictionnaire de la théologie catholique,* "Rédemption." Letouzey et Ané, 1920.

Sayés, J. A. *El Misterio eucaristico.* BAC, 1986.

Schillebeeckx, Edouard. *Le Christ, sacrement de la rencontre avec Dieu. Lex orandi.* Paris: Cerf, 1964.

Sorci, Pietro. *"Mistero pasquale."* NDL.

Vagaggini, Cyprien. *"La constitution de Vatican II sur la liturgie."* *Paroisse et liturgie*, 65, 1964.

Vagaggini, Cyprien. *Initiation à la théologie de la liturgie.* Bruges: Apostolat liturgique, 1959.

Wojtyla, Karol. *Aux sources du renouveau: étude sur la mise en oeuvre de Vatican II.* Centurion, 1979.